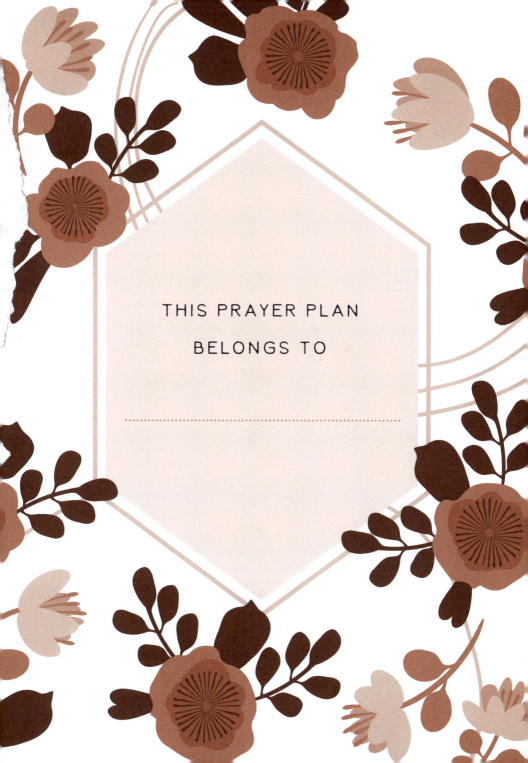

THIS PRAYER PLAN

BELONGS TO

....

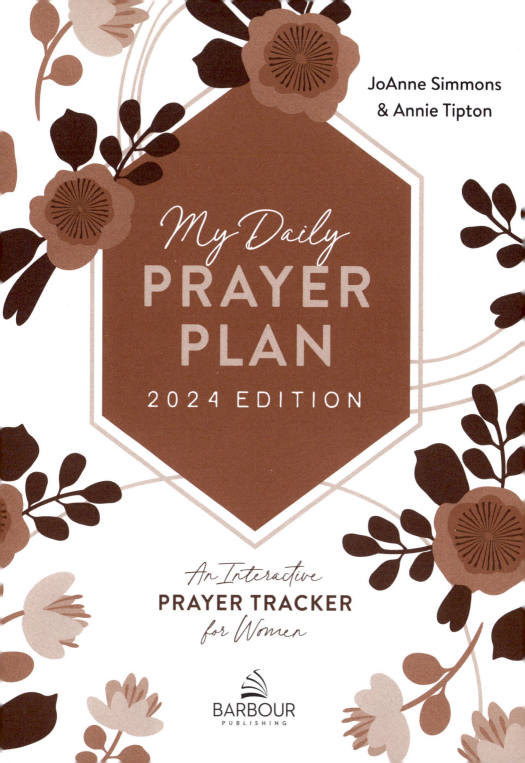

JoAnne Simmons
& Annie Tipton

My Daily
PRAYER
PLAN

2024 EDITION

An Interactive
PRAYER TRACKER
for Women

BARBOUR
PUBLISHING

© 2023 by Barbour Publishing, Inc.

ISBN 978-1-63609-621-6

Published by Barbour Publishing, Inc., 1810 Barbour Drive, Uhrichsville, Ohio 44683, www.barbourbooks.com

Our mission is to inspire the world with the life-changing message of the Bible.

Printed in China.

Welcome to

MY DAILY PRAYER PLAN: 2024 EDITION

What better way to start the new year than with a tool that can help your prayer life flourish in 2024? That's just what the book you hold in your hands can do.

Part Bible study, part daily devotional, part prayer journal, and part prayer tracker, this fantastic guide gives you everything you need to spend a few minutes every day in prayer. Each day includes a scripture and a short devotional prayer. Below that, you'll be able to write down what's on your own heart in a conversation with God. Don't worry about making your prayer perfect or eloquent. The Bible tells us that when we talk to God, He is faithful to listen to us (Jeremiah 29:12). At the bottom of the page are dedicated spots for your prayer requests, praises, and answers to prayer.

Each month begins with a full calendar page and follows an encouraging, challenging theme:

JANUARY – God Makes All Things New

FEBRUARY – Love, above All

MARCH – Experiencing Joy

APRIL – Cultivating Peace

MAY – Learning Patience

JUNE – Practicing Kindness

JULY – The Gift of Hope

AUGUST – A Foundation of Faithfulness

SEPTEMBER – Celebrating Daily Blessings

OCTOBER – Living a Courageous Life

NOVEMBER – Contentment and Gratitude

DECEMBER – When God Says "Wait"

At the end of 2024, you'll have a year's worth of reflections to look back on and see how God has worked in your life. May this year be the next step in your faith journey as you come to know your heavenly Father more intimately through prayer!

"When you pray, I will listen. If you look for me wholeheartedly, you will find me."
JEREMIAH 29:12–13 NLT

January

GOD MAKES ALL THINGS NEW

Make a clean heart in me, O God.
Give me a new spirit that will not be moved.
PSALM 51:10 NLV

SUNDAY	MONDAY	TUESDAY	WEDNESDAY	THURSDAY	FRIDAY	SATURDAY
	1 New Year's Day	2	3	4	5	6
7	8	9	10	11	12	13
14	15 Martin Luther King Jr. Day	16	17	18	19	20
21	22	23	24	25	26	27
28	29	30	31			

The turn of the calendar page from December to January often feels like a REFRESH button. And what better time to ask God to do something new in your life? After all, He is a God of transformation—He makes all things new, including Y-O-U!

MONDAY, JANUARY 1, 2024
New Year's Day

He put a new song in my mouth, a song of praise to our God.
PSALM 40:3 NLV

Almighty God, You have ushered in a new year, and I am singing a new song of praise. You are holy. You are good. You are righteous, and I trust You no matter what. You are what I need. Fill my moments, my hours, and my days with Your glory. Please lead me this year in expectant hope. I want more of Your grace, Your beauty, and Your love. . . .

PRAYER REQUESTS

ANSWERS TO PRAYER

PRAISES

TUESDAY, JANUARY 2

*Therefore, if anyone is in Christ, the new creation
has come: The old has gone, the new is here!*
2 CORINTHIANS 5:17 NIV

God, I am in awe of Your work in me. When I think of where I was before I came to know You and love You, I see how much I have changed. Today I am new, refreshed, and vibrant as I stand in the grace of Jesus Christ. I am loved, I am forgiven, I am whole, I am Your child. . . .

PRAYER REQUESTS

PRAISES

ANSWERS TO PRAYER

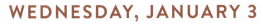

WEDNESDAY, JANUARY 3

He who sat on the throne said, "Behold, I make all things new."
REVELATION 21:5 SKJV

Father, open my eyes to see Your hand in the changes in me and around me. I want to live each day in anticipation of the new things You are doing. Give me insight into Your will, and please allow me to be a small part of Your work to shine Your light to everyone around me. I am willing, Lord! . . .

PRAYER REQUESTS

ANSWERS TO PRAYER

PRAISES

THURSDAY, JANUARY 4

Sing a new song to the LORD! Sing his
praises from the ends of the earth!
ISAIAH 42:10 NLT

I have a melody in my heart today, Lord. The words fill me with gratitude for all You are and all You are doing. You are a God of action, and I have faith that You are working everything together for my good, even when I don't see it. So my heart will continue to sing of Your greatness. . . .

PRAYER REQUESTS

PRAISES

ANSWERS TO PRAYER

FRIDAY, JANUARY 5

"I will give you a new heart and put a new spirit within you.
I will take away your heart of stone and give you a heart of flesh."
EZEKIEL 36:26 NLV

Holy Spirit, on days when my heart is hard, I need Your help more than usual. I know You have the power to change me—to remove that weight inside my chest and fill me with a heart that is attuned to God's glory. Give me a heart filled with love, today and every day. . . .

PRAYER REQUESTS

ANSWERS
TO PRAYER

PRAISES

SATURDAY, JANUARY 6

*The Holy Spirit raised Jesus from the dead. If the same Holy Spirit
lives in you, He will give life to your bodies in the same way.*
ROMANS 8:11 NLV

Father, some days the world makes me feel weak and useless. When that happens,
I need the Holy Spirit to spark in my heart and help me to realize that the power
that raised Jesus from death lives inside my heart. I am powerful in the Father,
the Son, and the Holy Spirit. . . .

PRAYER REQUESTS

PRAISES

ANSWERS TO PRAYER

SUNDAY, JANUARY 7

*Put on your new nature, created to be
like God—truly righteous and holy.*

EPHESIANS 4:24 NLT

Precious God, today I'm clothing myself with the new wardrobe You have created for me. I will take off my former nature and dress like You by putting on righteousness, holiness, love, joy, peace, patience, kindness, goodness, faithfulness, gentleness, and self-control. God, thank You for considering me worthy to wear such beautiful attire. Today, use me for Your good and perfect will. . . .

Help me to see you at work because so many days I am blind to what your will is and some days I want your will to be what I desire and it isn't. Help me to take You at Your word and be satisfied with what You say.

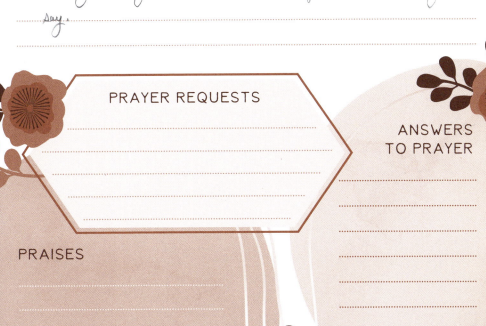

PRAYER REQUESTS

ANSWERS
TO PRAYER

PRAISES

MONDAY, JANUARY 8

"Forget the former things; do not dwell on the past. See, I am doing a new thing! Now it springs up; do you not perceive it? I am making a way in the wilderness and streams in the wasteland."

ISAIAH 43:18–19 NIV

Father, help me let go of my life before I knew You. Sometimes the guilt of my mistakes creeps back into my heart. Help me to forget the past and focus on the vibrant life ahead of me as I follow You. . . .

PRAYER REQUESTS

PRAISES

ANSWERS TO PRAYER

TUESDAY, JANUARY 9

*"I will give them an undivided heart and put a
new spirit in them; I will remove from them their
heart of stone and give them a heart of flesh."*
EZEKIEL 11:19 NIV

Jesus, my whole heart is Yours. This is the truth of my belief in You. When my vision strays away from You and to myself, when I feel my own selfish pride grow, strengthen Your Spirit inside of me so that I am focused only on You and Your perfect plan for me. . . .

PRAYER REQUESTS

ANSWERS
TO PRAYER

PRAISES

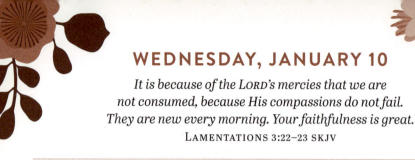

WEDNESDAY, JANUARY 10

*It is because of the LORD's mercies that we are
not consumed, because His compassions do not fail.
They are new every morning. Your faithfulness is great.*
LAMENTATIONS 3:22–23 SKJV

Creator God, I am so thankful that You usher in a new day every twenty-four hours. Both the freshness of each dawn and the daily grace You provide give me the courage I need to live purposefully for You. I will not waste today. Instead, I will...

PRAYER REQUESTS

PRAISES

ANSWERS TO PRAYER

THURSDAY, JANUARY 11

Let us thank the God and Father of our Lord Jesus Christ.
It was through His loving-kindness that we were born
again to a new life and have a hope that never dies. This
hope is ours because Jesus was raised from the dead.
1 PETER 1:3 NLV

Thank You, Jesus, for the unending daily hope You give me. That hope is my foundation to face the big challenges of life, and it's also the flame that allows me to shine Your light in a dark world. . . .

PRAYER REQUESTS

ANSWERS TO PRAYER

PRAISES

FRIDAY, JANUARY 12

"For I know the plans I have for you," says the Lord. "They are plans for good and not for disaster, to give you a future and a hope."
JEREMIAH 29:11 NLT

I surrender my future to You, Lord God. Because if I try to think about the unknown on my own, I get worried. You know what's going to happen, and I trust You. Your plan for my tomorrow is good and filled with hope. I want more of that. . . .

PRAYER REQUESTS

PRAISES

ANSWERS TO PRAYER

SATURDAY, JANUARY 13

"For behold, I create new heavens and a new earth, and the former shall not be remembered or come into mind."
Isaiah 65:17 SKJV

Father, help me to live fully present today but also with the hope of Your perfect eternity. Give me the strength to endure the challenges and heartaches now, knowing that You will make all things right and good and whole in the future. Thank You for being here now and being there already in tomorrow and forever....

PRAYER REQUESTS

ANSWERS TO PRAYER

PRAISES

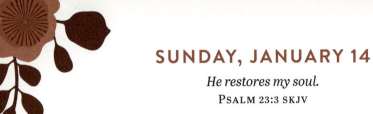

SUNDAY, JANUARY 14

He restores my soul.
PSALM 23:3 SKJV

You are an expert craftsman, God. Today, I come to You as a piece of shattered pottery with a chipped, dull finish. I'm broken, Father, and I can't fix myself. Although I don't deserve it, I ask You to restore me to be Your beautiful creation, formed in Your image. When You rebuild me through the grace of Jesus, I am better than just mended or rehabilitated. I am a new creation and I am whole. . . .

PRAYER REQUESTS

PRAISES

ANSWERS TO PRAYER

MONDAY, JANUARY 15

Martin Luther King Jr. Day

"He will wipe every tear from their eyes, and there will be no more death or sorrow or crying or pain. All these things are gone forever."

REVELATION 21:4 NLT

God of eternity, my soul longs for the time when there will be no more death. No more sorrow. No more crying. No more pain. While I wait for that time, help me to bring Your salvation to others so they can live in confident hope as well. . . .

PRAYER REQUESTS

ANSWERS TO PRAYER

PRAISES

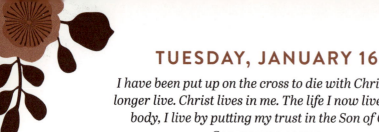

TUESDAY, JANUARY 16

I have been put up on the cross to die with Christ. I no longer live. Christ lives in me. The life I now live in this body, I live by putting my trust in the Son of God.
GALATIANS 2:20 NLV

I'm laying my whole self down today, Jesus. I'm no longer driven by my selfishness. You laid down Your life to save me, Lord, and now I am doing the same so that I can experience You more. I trust You with everything. . . .

PRAYER REQUESTS

PRAISES

ANSWERS TO PRAYER

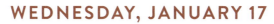

WEDNESDAY, JANUARY 17

"But forget all that—it is nothing compared to what I am going to do."
Isaiah 43:18 NLT

God, when I think about the ways You have brought me through difficult times in the past, I'm amazed and deeply grateful. But You tell me You've got even bigger and better things for the future. What exceptional things are You doing, God? Will You let me see behind the curtain as You move powerfully, working things together for the good of Your children? . . .

PRAYER REQUESTS

ANSWERS TO PRAYER

PRAISES

THURSDAY, JANUARY 18

And after you have suffered a little while, the God of all grace, who has called you to his eternal glory in Christ, will himself restore, confirm, strengthen, and establish you.

1 PETER 5:10 ESV

There are days that feel impossible to handle, Jesus. When I'm struggling, help me to remember that these frustrating circumstances are only temporary. The one thing that is eternal is You—and Your power to set me on solid ground and make me whole. . . .

PRAYER REQUESTS

PRAISES

ANSWERS TO PRAYER

FRIDAY, JANUARY 19

We know that God makes all things work together for the good of those who love Him and are chosen to be a part of His plan.
ROMANS 8:28 NLV

Father, I know I only understand a tiny part of what You are doing in my life right now, and some things just don't make sense to me! But I choose to hold on to Your promise that the ways You are working, the details You spell out, are all weaving together a tapestry of goodness. . . .

PRAYER REQUESTS

ANSWERS TO PRAYER

PRAISES

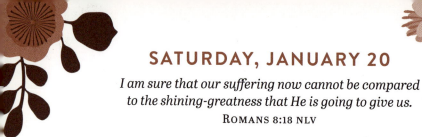

SATURDAY, JANUARY 20

I am sure that our suffering now cannot be compared to the shining-greatness that He is going to give us.

ROMANS 8:18 NLV

Almighty God, what does tomorrow hold? You know the answer to that question for all my tomorrows. My curiosity and eager hope grow as each day passes. I believe Your best is yet to come—and Your best is the greatest gift I can receive. Thank You for helping me push through today to get to tomorrow. . . .

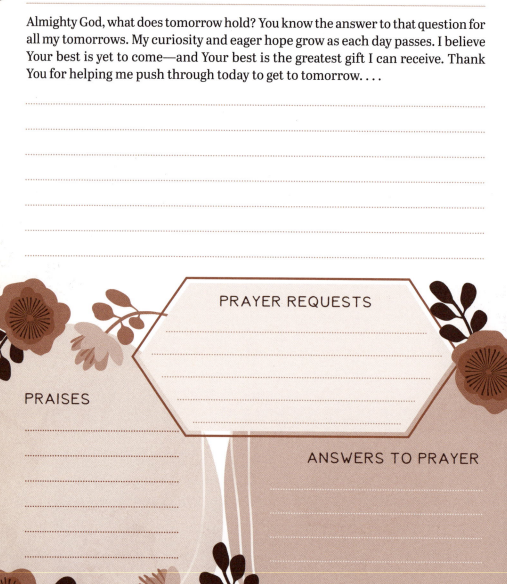

PRAYER REQUESTS

PRAISES

ANSWERS TO PRAYER

SUNDAY, JANUARY 21

Therefore, there is now no condemnation
for those who are in Christ Jesus.
ROMANS 8:1 NIV

I admit that I am sometimes afraid of the punishment I deserve for the mistakes I make, Jesus. The truth is I *should* get what I deserve. But Your Word tells me that because You call me sister, I am not condemned. I am covered in the grace of Your forgiveness, and I am loved. Thank You for saving me from the judgment I should rightfully receive. . . .

PRAYER REQUESTS

ANSWERS TO PRAYER

PRAISES

MONDAY, JANUARY 22

*Put on your new nature, and be renewed as you
learn to know your Creator and become like him.*
COLOSSIANS 3:10 NLT

I am a new person, crafted by Your expert hand, creator God. You've taken away my old sinful nature, and this new nature has room to grow and mature. Teach me, Father, to be more like Jesus in my actions, words, and thoughts. Help me to love others more fully. Make the Holy Spirit come alive in my heart today. . . .

PRAYER REQUESTS

PRAISES

ANSWERS TO PRAYER

TUESDAY, JANUARY 23

In the beginning God created the heaven and the earth.
GENESIS 1:1 SKJV

Thank You, God, for being a creator who loves to do new things. You cherish new life and deeper growth and thriving creation, and I reap the benefits of every beginning You usher forth. I want to foster that same new birth in my life, Father. When I see the chance to start something new in Your name, help me to begin. I am here, Lord, willing and able. . . .

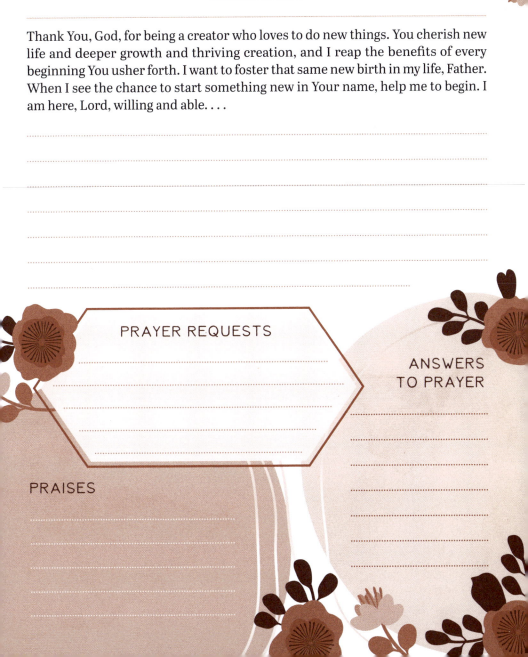

PRAYER REQUESTS

ANSWERS TO PRAYER

PRAISES

WEDNESDAY, JANUARY 24

The Word (Christ) was in the beginning.
The Word was with God. The Word was God.
JOHN 1:1 NLV

I am awestruck by the idea of eternity, God. In eternity past and eternity future, You are there. I get so distracted by my here and now that I lose sight of Your immense power of simply *being*. I trust You with my past, I trust You with my now, and I trust You with my forever. Be the Lord of my whole being. . . .

PRAYER REQUESTS

PRAISES

ANSWERS TO PRAYER

THURSDAY, JANUARY 25

Like newborn babies, crave pure spiritual milk,
so that by it you may grow up in your salvation.
1 PETER 2:2 NIV

I want to mature in my faith, Father! Help me to seek out the spiritual nourishment I need to grow more like Jesus each day. I will plant seeds of Your Word in my heart so they can take root and I will grow stronger and sturdier in my knowledge and belief. Bring into my life spiritual mentors who I can learn from. . . .

PRAYER REQUESTS

ANSWERS TO PRAYER

PRAISES

FRIDAY, JANUARY 26

"I am the Alpha and the Omega," says the Lord God,
"who is, and who was, and who is to come, the Almighty."
REVELATION 1:8 NIV

I take comfort in knowing You are already ahead of me, Lord. I'm often afraid of the future because it's unknown to me, but it is fully known and planned by You! Encourage me to faithfully step forward on Your path every day, knowing that You are there all along the way. . . .

PRAYER REQUESTS

PRAISES

ANSWERS TO PRAYER

SATURDAY, JANUARY 27

God showed his great love for us by sending
Christ to die for us while we were still sinners.
ROMANS 5:8 NLT

While I was still a sinner, You died for me, Jesus. You laid down Your life not because I was worthy but because You love me. You loved me before I accepted Your gift of grace. You love me now when I fail to live up to Your standard. You love me through forgiveness that covers today and tomorrow. Thank You. . . .

PRAYER REQUESTS

ANSWERS
TO PRAYER

PRAISES

SUNDAY, JANUARY 28

*"May your Kingdom come soon. May your
will be done on earth, as it is in heaven."*
MATTHEW 6:10 NLT

My heart is for Your kingdom, Lord. Please give me work to do that will make Your kingdom grow and will further Your plans on earth. If there are roadblocks in my heart that keep me from being effective, change me, Father. I want to help bring heaven to earth now, to be a beacon of Your light in the darkness. . . .

PRAYER REQUESTS

PRAISES

ANSWERS TO PRAYER

MONDAY, JANUARY 29

And my God will give you everything you need
because of His great riches in Christ Jesus.
PHILIPPIANS 4:19 NLV

Father, I trust You to supply all that I need here on earth and forever in heaven. Help me to recognize the difference between my needs and wants. Supply me with an abundance of grace, love, protection, wisdom, and a willing heart that is in tune with Your will. Cultivate a spirit of contentment and gratitude in me. . . .

PRAYER REQUESTS

ANSWERS TO PRAYER

PRAISES

TUESDAY, JANUARY 30

"As the heavens are higher than the earth, so are my ways higher than your ways and my thoughts than your thoughts."

ISAIAH 55:9 NIV

Sometimes, Your actions are much different than mine would be, Lord. But rather than letting the details of Your will confuse or frustrate me, I am thankful that You have the big-picture view of all of time and creation and that You know better than I do. Give me peace and the patience to wait for understanding. . . .

PRAYER REQUESTS

PRAISES

ANSWERS TO PRAYER

WEDNESDAY, JANUARY 31

God is able to do much more than we ask or
think through His power working in us.
EPHESIANS 3:20 NLV

I believe You are a big God! I believe You move and work mightily and powerfully. But I also know that You are more capable and more immense than my mind can understand. So I give You everything, God—all I am and all I can be. Work through me to do *more* than I ask and *more* than I imagine is even possible! . . .

PRAYER REQUESTS

ANSWERS
TO PRAYER

PRAISES

February

LOVE, ABOVE ALL

But the greatest of these is love.

1 Corinthians 13:13 NLV

SUNDAY	MONDAY	TUESDAY	WEDNESDAY	THURSDAY	FRIDAY	SATURDAY
				1	2	3
4	5	6	7	8	9	10
11	12	13	14 Valentine's Day Ash Wednesday	15	16	17
18	19 Presidents' Day	20	21	22	23	24
25	26	27	28	29 Leap Day		

Scripture tells us that God is the author of love; He is love itself. If people know how to love and bless others, then how much more does God? Immeasurably, infinitely more! He is your Creator and heavenly Father. And as you are filled with His great love, let it overflow from you to others.

THURSDAY, FEBRUARY 1

*Dear friends, let us love each other, because love comes from God.
Those who love are God's children and they know God. Those
who do not love do not know God because God is love. God has
shown His love to us by sending His only Son into the world.*

1 JOHN 4:7–9 NLV

Heavenly Father, remind me every day who I am—Your child. I know You, I know
You are real love, and I want to know You more. Please help me to show love to
others in ways that imitate Your great love. . . .

PRAYER REQUESTS

ANSWERS TO PRAYER

PRAISES

FRIDAY, FEBRUARY 2

God has chosen you. You are holy and loved by Him.
Because of this, your new life should be full of loving-pity.
You should be kind to others and have no pride.
COLOSSIANS 3:12 NLV

Almighty God, it is only by Your mercy and grace that I am loved and able to truly love others. Thank You for choosing me and giving me new, wonderful, eternal life. Keep me so humble and full of gratitude toward You that I cannot help but give grace and mercy and love to everyone around me. . . .

PRAYER REQUESTS

PRAISES

ANSWERS TO PRAYER

SATURDAY, FEBRUARY 3

Let us not love with words or in talk only.
Let us love by what we do and in truth.
1 JOHN 3:18 NLV

Jesus, You didn't speak with empty, meaningless words. You proved Your message; You proved Your great love for me and for all who trust in You by giving Your life to save us from our sin. I want to keep on learning from Your sacrificial love. Please help my life to be an example of it, to point others to salvation and eternal life in You. . . .

PRAYER REQUESTS

ANSWERS TO PRAYER

PRAISES

SUNDAY, FEBRUARY 4

Be gentle and be willing to wait for others. Try to understand other people. Forgive each other. If you have something against someone, forgive him. That is the way the Lord forgave you. And to all these things, you must add love. Love holds everything and everybody together and makes all these good things perfect.
COLOSSIANS 3:12–14 NLV

I too easily forget these straightforward, practical ways to love people, Lord. Please help me to remember to be gentle, patient, understanding, and forgiving—just like You are with me every single day. . . .

PRAYER REQUESTS

PRAISES

ANSWERS TO PRAYER

MONDAY, FEBRUARY 5

Above all, love each other deeply,
because love covers over a multitude of sins.
1 PETER 4:8 NIV

On my worst days, and even on my best days, I desperately need the truth and peace found in this scripture, Father. I'm so grateful that Your love covers my multitude of sins. And because of this example You've given Your children, we can love each other deeply and forgive each other graciously and generously too. . . .

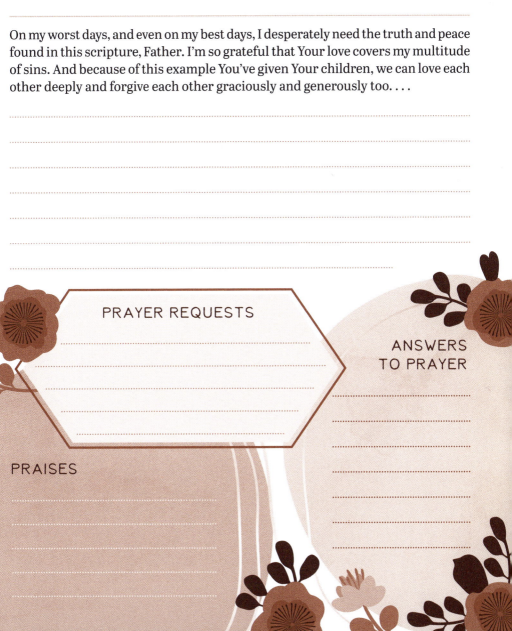

PRAYER REQUESTS

ANSWERS
TO PRAYER

PRAISES

TUESDAY, FEBRUARY 6

Let all that you do be done in love.

1 CORINTHIANS 16:14 ESV

Father, I don't obey this scripture enough, and I'm sorry. Please forgive me when my actions are so often not done in love for others; instead, I do them for my own selfish interests. Please increase my love for others as I grow in knowledge and awareness of Your great love for me. . . .

PRAYER REQUESTS

PRAISES

ANSWERS TO PRAYER

WEDNESDAY, FEBRUARY 7

"For God so loved the world, that he gave his only Son,
that whoever believes in him should not perish but have eternal life."
JOHN 3:16 ESV

Father, Your greatest gift of love was sending Your Son to save all people who believe in Him and to give them eternal life. I want to be constantly pointing people to that truth. Please use me to help others come to salvation through Jesus Christ. . . .

PRAYER REQUESTS

ANSWERS
TO PRAYER

PRAISES

THURSDAY, FEBRUARY 8

God shows his love for us in that while
we were still sinners, Christ died for us.
ROMANS 5:8 ESV

Heavenly Father, I'm so grateful that no one has to pretend to be perfect before coming to saving faith in You. While we were still sinners, Christ died for us all, and we only need to believe and accept His gift of grace and mercy. Now that my sin has been washed away, I want to do my best to live a life that honors You and shows my gratitude and love for You. . . .

PRAYER REQUESTS

PRAISES

ANSWERS TO PRAYER

FRIDAY, FEBRUARY 9

If I had the gift of prophecy, and if I understood all of God's secret plans and possessed all knowledge, and if I had such faith that I could move mountains, but didn't love others, I would be nothing. If I gave everything I have to the poor and even sacrificed my body, I could boast about it; but if I didn't love others, I would have gained nothing.

1 Corinthians 13:2–3 nlt

Lord, please help me to never just learn about Your love and talk about Your love. Help me to actively share Your great love with others. . . .

PRAYER REQUESTS

ANSWERS TO PRAYER

PRAISES

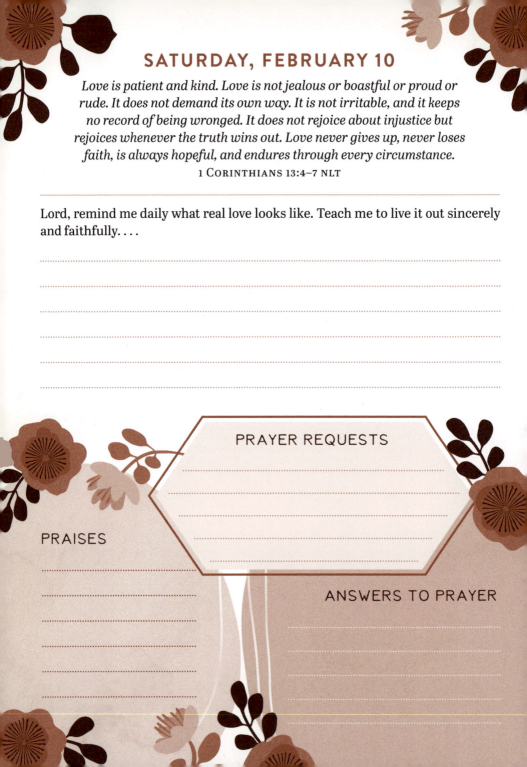

SATURDAY, FEBRUARY 10

Love is patient and kind. Love is not jealous or boastful or proud or rude. It does not demand its own way. It is not irritable, and it keeps no record of being wronged. It does not rejoice about injustice but rejoices whenever the truth wins out. Love never gives up, never loses faith, is always hopeful, and endures through every circumstance.

1 CORINTHIANS 13:4–7 NLT

Lord, remind me daily what real love looks like. Teach me to live it out sincerely and faithfully. . . .

PRAYER REQUESTS

PRAISES

ANSWERS TO PRAYER

SUNDAY, FEBRUARY 11

"Master, which is the great commandment in the law?"
Jesus said to him, "'You shall love the Lord your God with all
your heart, and with all your soul, and with all your mind.'
This is the first and great commandment. And the second
is like it: 'You shall love your neighbor as yourself.'"

MATTHEW 22:36–39 SKJV

Jesus, thank You for the simplicity and clarity of Your words here. Life is all about love. May my deepest and best love be for the one true God, and from that constantly growing relationship, may love overflow in my relationships with those around me. . . .

PRAYER REQUESTS

ANSWERS TO PRAYER

PRAISES

MONDAY, FEBRUARY 12

A friend loves at all times. A brother is born to share troubles.
PROVERBS 17:17 NLV

Thank You for the precious friendships You have blessed me with, Lord. Some friends come and go with various seasons of life, but the ones who stick through all kinds of joys and troubles are a true treasure. Please help me to love my friends and nurture relationships with them like You want me to. Help us to mutually encourage, bless, and support each other. . . .

PRAYER REQUESTS

PRAISES

ANSWERS TO PRAYER

TUESDAY, FEBRUARY 13

Those who won't care for their relatives, especially those in their own household, have denied the true faith.
1 TIMOTHY 5:8 NLT

Lord, help me to love, honor, value, and care for my family in ways that please You and bring glory to You. Thank You for Your good design for families. Even when conflicts and trials arise, we can look to You for examples of forgiveness and mercy. Please bless us—and help us to have so much fun together too! . . .

PRAYER REQUESTS

ANSWERS TO PRAYER

PRAISES

WEDNESDAY, FEBRUARY 14
Valentine's Day/Ash Wednesday

*See how very much our Father loves us, for he
calls us his children, and that is what we are!*

1 JOHN 3:1 NLT

Father, I'm so grateful for the best and most meaningful relationship in my life—the
one I have with You! You are the one true almighty God, King of kings and Lord
of lords, and the fact that You call me Your child is an indescribable blessing. Let
every other relationship in my life be filled with love that comes first and foremost
from my relationship with You. . . .

PRAYER REQUESTS

PRAISES

ANSWERS TO PRAYER

THURSDAY, FEBRUARY 15

"If you love me, you will keep my commandments. And I will ask the Father, and he will give you another Helper, to be with you forever, even the Spirit of truth.... You know him, for he dwells with you and will be in you."

JOHN 14:15–17 ESV

Jesus, I want to show You my love for You by keeping Your commandments as You've instructed. Thank You that I don't have to do that on my own. Thank You that I have the Holy Spirit always with me, helping me to obey Your Word....

PRAYER REQUESTS

ANSWERS TO PRAYER

PRAISES

FRIDAY, FEBRUARY 16

Neither death nor life, neither angels nor demons, neither the present nor the future, nor any powers, neither height nor depth, nor anything else in all creation, will be able to separate us from the love of God that is in Christ Jesus our Lord.

ROMANS 8:38–39 NIV

On the days I'm full of fear or anxiety or sadness (or all of the above and more)—those days I feel like I have no love to give—Lord, remind me that there is not a single thing of this world that can ever separate me from Your incredible love. . . .

PRAYER REQUESTS

PRAISES

ANSWERS TO PRAYER

SATURDAY, FEBRUARY 17

But you, Lord, are a compassionate and gracious God,
slow to anger, abounding in love and faithfulness.
PSALM 86:15 NIV

Heavenly Father, please help me to follow Your perfect example of being compassionate and gracious. When I fail at this, please forgive me and let those I've hurt forgive me and let me try again. Help me to abound in love and faithfulness toward others, like You do. . . .

PRAYER REQUESTS

ANSWERS
TO PRAYER

PRAISES

SUNDAY, FEBRUARY 18

Don't just pretend to love others. Really love them. Hate what is wrong. Hold tightly to what is good. Love each other with genuine affection, and take delight in honoring each other.

ROMANS 12:9–10 NLT

I don't want my love for others to be fake, Lord. Please forgive me for the times I've been disingenuous. Fill me with real love—Your love. Fill me with joy that comes from sincerely showing affection, care, and honor to others. . . .

PRAYER REQUESTS

PRAISES

ANSWERS TO PRAYER

MONDAY, FEBRUARY 19

Presidents' Day

Your unfailing love is better than life itself; how I praise
you! I will praise you as long as I live, lifting up my
hands to you in prayer. You satisfy me more than the
richest feast. I will praise you with songs of joy.

PSALM 63:3–5 NLT

Yes, Lord, I have experienced how Your unfailing love is better than life itself! I sing praise to You and come to You in prayer, eager to talk with You and hear from You and learn from You. . . .

PRAYER REQUESTS

ANSWERS TO PRAYER

PRAISES

TUESDAY, FEBRUARY 20

The fruit of the Spirit is love, joy, peace, patience,
kindness, goodness, faithfulness, gentleness,
self-control; against such things there is no law.
GALATIANS 5:22–23 ESV

Grow the fruit of the Spirit in my life, please, Lord. Let it be abundant! As I live for You and learn from You, I pray it will be evident to all who know me that You have made me full of love, joy, peace, patience, kindness, goodness, faithfulness, gentleness, and self-control. . . .

PRAYER REQUESTS

PRAISES

ANSWERS TO PRAYER

WEDNESDAY, FEBRUARY 21

*Give thanks to the L*ORD*, for he is good. His love endures forever.*
Give thanks to the God of gods. His love endures forever. Give
thanks to the Lord of lords: His love endures forever.

PSALM 136:1–3 NIV

Sometimes I just need to hear it on repeat, Lord—Your love endures forever. Thank You for Your promise again and again that Your love never ends. I give thanks and praise to You for all You are and all You do! . . .

PRAYER REQUESTS

ANSWERS TO PRAYER

PRAISES

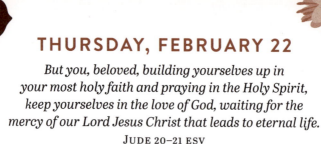

THURSDAY, FEBRUARY 22

*But you, beloved, building yourselves up in
your most holy faith and praying in the Holy Spirit,
keep yourselves in the love of God, waiting for the
mercy of our Lord Jesus Christ that leads to eternal life.*

JUDE 20–21 ESV

Heavenly Father, I want to keep myself in Your love, staying in close relationship with You! Please forgive me for the times I have forgotten and ignored You. I never want to do that again. . . .

PRAYER REQUESTS

PRAISES

ANSWERS TO PRAYER

FRIDAY, FEBRUARY 23

Be careful that you do not please your old selves by sinning because you are free. Live this free life by loving and helping others.
GALATIANS 5:13 NLV

Lord, thank You for the freedom I have because You have saved me from sin. But I don't ever want to take that for granted. Help me to avoid and flee from sin. Let my life be focused not on myself and my freedom but on loving and helping others every chance I get. . . .

PRAYER REQUESTS

ANSWERS
TO PRAYER

PRAISES

SATURDAY, FEBRUARY 24

I love you, LORD, my strength. The LORD is my rock, my fortress and my deliverer; my God is my rock, in whom I take refuge, my shield and the horn of my salvation, my stronghold.

PSALM 18:1–2 NIV

Lord, I don't always feel like I have the power or endurance or energy to keep on loving others the way You ask me to. So I'm thankful I'm not depending on myself. You are my strength and my rock and my stronghold. . . .

PRAYER REQUESTS

PRAISES

ANSWERS TO PRAYER

SUNDAY, FEBRUARY 25

Make every effort to add to your faith goodness; and to goodness, knowledge; and to knowledge, self-control; and to self-control, perseverance; and to perseverance, godliness; and to godliness, mutual affection; and to mutual affection, love. For if you possess these qualities in increasing measure, they will keep you from being ineffective and unproductive in your knowledge of our Lord Jesus Christ.

2 PETER 1:5–8 NIV

Lord Jesus, please help me to keep adding to my faith so that I can be effective and productive in bringing You glory. . . .

PRAYER REQUESTS

ANSWERS TO PRAYER

PRAISES

MONDAY, FEBRUARY 26

Live and work the way the Lord expected you to live and work.
Live and work without pride. Be gentle and kind. Do not be hard on
others. Let love keep you from doing that. Work hard to live together
as one by the help of the Holy Spirit. Then there will be peace.
EPHESIANS 4:1–3 NLV

Lord, please help me to live in loving, peaceful community with other believers as You intended. Let our love and care for each other be a testimony to those who do not yet know You as Savior. . . .

PRAYER REQUESTS

PRAISES

ANSWERS TO PRAYER

TUESDAY, FEBRUARY 27

"You have heard the law that says, 'Love your neighbor' and hate your enemy. But I say, love your enemies! Pray for those who persecute you! In that way, you will be acting as true children of your Father in heaven."
MATTHEW 5:43–45 NLT

This is no easy command to obey, Jesus. But I want to do my best at this with Your help. It's only with Your mercy and power that I can pray for and love and bless my enemies. . . .

PRAYER REQUESTS

ANSWERS TO PRAYER

PRAISES

WEDNESDAY, FEBRUARY 28

God's love has been poured into our hearts through the Holy Spirit who has been given to us.

ROMANS 5:5 ESV

Thank You for giving me the Holy Spirit, Lord! Remind me that Your love has been poured generously into my heart. I am lost without You. I desperately need Your love every moment of my life, along with the protection, strength, confidence, and guidance Your Holy Spirit gives me. . . .

PRAYER REQUESTS

PRAISES

ANSWERS TO PRAYER

THURSDAY, FEBRUARY 29

Leap Day

*Let the morning bring me word of your unfailing love, for I
have put my trust in you. Show me the way I should go,
for to you I entrust my life. Rescue me from my enemies, Lord,
for I hide myself in you. Teach me to do your will, for you are
my God; may your good Spirit lead me on level ground.*

PSALM 143:8–10 NIV

I trust in You alone, Lord! Your love for me never ever fails. Help me to remember
that. Teach me to love more and to do Your will. . . .

PRAYER REQUESTS

ANSWERS
TO PRAYER

PRAISES

March

EXPERIENCING JOY

Though you have not seen [Jesus Christ], you love him;
and even though you do not see him now, you believe in him
and are filled with an inexpressible and glorious joy, for you are
receiving the end result of your faith, the salvation of your souls.

1 PETER 1:8–9 NIV

SUNDAY	MONDAY	TUESDAY	WEDNESDAY	THURSDAY	FRIDAY	SATURDAY
					1	2
3	4	5	6	7	8	9
10 Daylight Saving Time Begins	11	12	13	14	15	16
17 St. Patrick's Day	18	19 First Day of Spring	20	21	22	23
24 Palm Sunday Easter 31	25	26	27	28	29 Good Friday	30

Happy feelings come and go in this life. But for the Christian, real joy comes from knowing and loving Jesus Christ as Savior. Let God's Word stir up that joy inside you every single day!

FRIDAY, MARCH 1

Be full of joy always because you belong to the Lord. Again I say,
be full of joy! ... Do not worry. Learn to pray about everything.
Give thanks to God as you ask Him for what you need. The peace
of God is much greater than the human mind can understand. This
peace will keep your hearts and minds through Christ Jesus.

PHILIPPIANS 4:4, 6–7 NLV

Lord, too often I forget my joy in belonging to You because I let worry consume
me. I want to bring my anxious thoughts to You and let Your peace and joy replace
them. . . .

PRAYER REQUESTS

ANSWERS
TO PRAYER

PRAISES

SATURDAY, MARCH 2

This is the day that the Lord has made.
Let us be full of joy and be glad in it.
PSALM 118:24 NLV

There is not a day that goes by that You have not ordained, Lord. No matter my circumstances, I want to remember that Your timing and plans are perfect. You are sovereign and good, and all my hope is in You. I rejoice and praise You with all my heart! . . .

PRAYER REQUESTS

PRAISES

ANSWERS TO PRAYER

SUNDAY, MARCH 3

A joyful heart is good medicine,
but a crushed spirit dries up the bones.
PROVERBS 17:22 ESV

Thank You so much for laughter and fun, Lord. Remind me that it's good medicine—so good for my health to be full of joy. When it's tempting to let sadness and worry overtake me, remind me that those feelings will only destroy my mental health and, eventually, my physical health too. I have every reason to be full of joy—even when life is hard—because of Your gift of salvation and eternal life! . . .

PRAYER REQUESTS

ANSWERS
TO PRAYER

PRAISES

MONDAY, MARCH 4

"I have loved you even as the Father has loved me. Remain in my love. When you obey my commandments, you remain in my love, just as I obey my Father's commandments and remain in his love. I have told you these things so that you will be filled with my joy. Yes, your joy will overflow!"

JOHN 15:9–11 NLT

Jesus, I don't want to forget this: when I obey Your commands, I remain in Your love, and when I remain in Your love, my joy will overflow. . . .

PRAYER REQUESTS

PRAISES

ANSWERS TO PRAYER

TUESDAY, MARCH 5

For the kingdom of God is not a matter of eating and drinking
but of righteousness and peace and joy in the Holy Spirit.
ROMANS 14:17 ESV

I'm so grateful to be part of Your kingdom, God! Thank You for eternal life! Thank You for the Holy Spirit living in me! Thank You for the righteousness, peace, and joy that can never be taken from me. . . .

PRAYER REQUESTS

ANSWERS TO PRAYER

PRAISES

WEDNESDAY, MARCH 6

May the God of hope fill you with all joy and peace as you trust in him,
so that you may overflow with hope by the power of the Holy Spirit.
ROMANS 15:13 NIV

Please forgive me when I choose not to trust in You, God. I realize that's what steals a lot of my joy. I believe You fill me with joy and peace when I focus on every reason I have to trust You to take care of all my needs. You always have in the past, and You will continue today and in the future. . . .

PRAYER REQUESTS

PRAISES

ANSWERS TO PRAYER

THURSDAY, MARCH 7

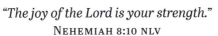

"The joy of the Lord is your strength."
NEHEMIAH 8:10 NLV

Real joy is powerful! Help me not to forget that, Lord. Your joy is my strength through every sorrow and sadness, every trial and pain. . . .

PRAYER REQUESTS

ANSWERS TO PRAYER

PRAISES

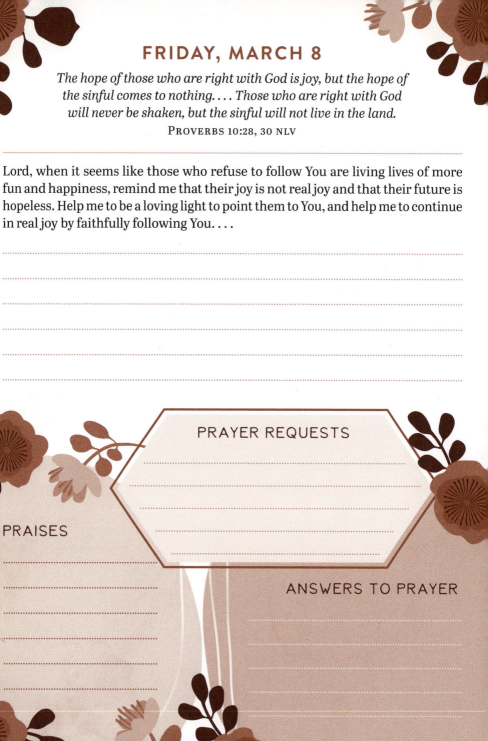

FRIDAY, MARCH 8

The hope of those who are right with God is joy, but the hope of the sinful comes to nothing. . . . Those who are right with God will never be shaken, but the sinful will not live in the land.

PROVERBS 10:28, 30 NLV

Lord, when it seems like those who refuse to follow You are living lives of more fun and happiness, remind me that their joy is not real joy and that their future is hopeless. Help me to be a loving light to point them to You, and help me to continue in real joy by faithfully following You. . . .

PRAYER REQUESTS

PRAISES

ANSWERS TO PRAYER

SATURDAY, MARCH 9

I have placed the Lord always in front of me. Because He is at my right hand, I will not be moved. And so my heart is glad. My soul is full of joy.... You will show me the way of life. Being with You is to be full of joy. In Your right hand there is happiness forever.

PSALM 16:8–9, 11 NLV

It's so awesome that You are right here with me, Lord! You are the one true almighty God, King of kings and Lord of lords, and I am Your child—wow! Your love for me amazes me....

PRAYER REQUESTS

ANSWERS TO PRAYER

PRAISES

SUNDAY, MARCH 10

Daylight Saving Time Begins

"But ask the wild animals, and they will teach you. Ask the birds of the heavens, and let them tell you. Or speak to the earth, and let it teach you. Let the fish of the sea make it known to you. Who among all these does not know that the hand of the Lord has done this? In His hand is the life of every living thing and the breath of all men."

JOB 12:7–10 NLV

Your creation astounds me, Father! Thank You for the joy You give through the beauty of animals and the natural world around me. . . .

PRAYER REQUESTS

PRAISES

ANSWERS TO PRAYER

MONDAY, MARCH 11

*O my God, I will praise You with a harp. I will praise Your
truth. I will sing praises to You with different kinds of
harps, O Holy One of Israel. My lips will call out for joy
when I sing praises to You. You have set my soul free.*

PSALM 71:22–23 NLV

If I forget my joy in You, God, please remind me to make music and sing praise to
You. Then my heart and mind will be in the right place again—focused on You,
where real joy is found. . . .

PRAYER REQUESTS

ANSWERS TO PRAYER

PRAISES

TUESDAY, MARCH 12

Bless those who persecute you. Don't curse them; pray that God will bless them. Be happy with those who are happy, and weep with those who weep. Live in harmony with each other. Don't be too proud to enjoy the company of ordinary people. And don't think you know it all! Never pay back evil with more evil. Do things in such a way that everyone can see you are honorable. Do all that you can to live in peace with everyone.

ROMANS 12:14–18 NLT

Lord, please let me have great joy in my life as I live in good relationship with others the way You want me to. . . .

PRAYER REQUESTS

PRAISES

ANSWERS TO PRAYER

WEDNESDAY, MARCH 13

Let us run with perseverance the race marked out for us, fixing our eyes on Jesus, the pioneer and perfecter of faith. For the joy set before him he endured the cross, scorning its shame, and sat down at the right hand of the throne of God. Consider him who endured such opposition from sinners, so that you will not grow weary and lose heart.
HEBREWS 12:1–3 NIV

You could endure the suffering of the cross because of the joy set before You, Jesus! I know there is incredible joy awaiting me in heaven, and joy along the way too, so please help me to run well this race in life You have marked out for me. . . .

PRAYER REQUESTS

ANSWERS TO PRAYER

PRAISES

THURSDAY, MARCH 14

Rejoice in hope, be patient in tribulation, be constant in prayer.
ROMANS 12:12 ESV

I have incredible joy because of my real hope in You, Lord! You are my Savior from sin, and nothing can separate me from Your love and gift of eternal life. So, I will choose to be patient in the midst of whatever trial I'm facing today. I'll be constant in my prayers to You. . . .

PRAYER REQUESTS

PRAISES

ANSWERS TO PRAYER

FRIDAY, MARCH 15

*Dear friends, don't be surprised at the fiery trials you are
going through, as if something strange were happening to you.
Instead, be very glad—for these trials make you partners with
Christ in his suffering, so that you will have the wonderful
joy of seeing his glory when it is revealed to all the world.*

1 PETER 4:12–13 NLT

Jesus, remind me that I am a partner with You when I am suffering through various
trials. Help me to focus on my joy in You, despite my earthly circumstances. I trust
You will make all things right in all the world one day soon! . . .

PRAYER REQUESTS

ANSWERS TO PRAYER

PRAISES

SATURDAY, MARCH 16

Take delight in the LORD, and he will give you the desires of your heart. Commit your way to the LORD; trust in him and he will do this: He will make your righteous reward shine like the dawn, your vindication like the noonday sun.

PSALM 37:4–6 NIV

Lord, when my delight is in You, I will want Your will most of all. And when I want Your will most of all, You are happy to give me the desires of my heart. You fill me with joy as I commit my way to You. . . .

PRAYER REQUESTS

PRAISES

ANSWERS TO PRAYER

SUNDAY, MARCH 17

St. Patrick's Day

Call out with joy to the Lord, all the earth. Be glad as you serve the Lord. Come before Him with songs of joy. Know that the Lord is God. It is He Who made us, and not we ourselves. We are His people and the sheep of His field. Go into His gates giving thanks and into His holy place with praise. Give thanks to Him. Honor His name.

PSALM 100:1–4 NLV

Worshipping You fills me with joy, Lord! I thank and praise You for who You are and the many ways I see You working. . . .

PRAYER REQUESTS

ANSWERS TO PRAYER

PRAISES

MONDAY, MARCH 18

Let all who put their trust in You be glad. Let them sing with joy forever. You make a covering for them, that all who love Your name may be glad in You. For You will make those happy who do what is right, O Lord. You will cover them all around with Your favor.

PSALM 5:11–12 NLV

I trust in You, Lord, and therefore I can sing with joy forever. You cover and protect me; I have nothing to fear. I praise and thank You for Your loving favor....

PRAYER REQUESTS

PRAISES

ANSWERS TO PRAYER

TUESDAY, MARCH 19

First Day of Spring

*The Lord your God is with you, a Powerful One Who wins the
battle. He will have much joy over you. With His love He will
give you new life. He will have joy over you with loud singing.*

ZEPHANIAH 3:17 NLV

As I rejoice in my hope in You, Lord, it's neat to think about how You take great
joy in Your people too. I want to honor You and bring You joy in all that I do for all
of my life. . . .

PRAYER REQUESTS

ANSWERS TO PRAYER

PRAISES

WEDNESDAY, MARCH 20

When I said, "My foot is slipping," your unfailing love, Lord, supported me. When anxiety was great within me, your consolation brought me joy.
PSALM 94:18–19 NIV

Thank You for always supporting me with Your unfailing love, Lord. Even when I'm worried and fearful, full of anxiety, I trust You will comfort and console me and fill me with joy again. . . .

PRAYER REQUESTS

PRAISES

ANSWERS TO PRAYER

THURSDAY, MARCH 21

*Your Word have I hid in my heart, that I may not sin against You.
. . . I have found as much joy in following Your Law as one finds
in much riches. I will think about Your Law and have respect for
Your ways. I will be glad in Your Law. I will not forget Your Word.*

PSALM 119:11, 14–16 NLV

Lord, I want this to be so true of me—that following Your Word gives me as much joy as great riches. Help me to hide Your Word in my heart and delight in it. . . .

PRAYER REQUESTS

ANSWERS
TO PRAYER

PRAISES

FRIDAY, MARCH 22

Consider it pure joy, my brothers and sisters, whenever you face trials of many kinds, because you know that the testing of your faith produces perseverance. Let perseverance finish its work so that you may be mature and complete, not lacking anything.

JAMES 1:2–4 NIV

Lord, it's hard to consider it joy when I'm facing trials—really hard! Help me to remember why I should: Your Word says that the trials and testing of my faith produce perseverance and that when perseverance finishes its work, I'll be mature and complete, not lacking anything. I love and trust You, Lord. . . .

PRAYER REQUESTS

PRAISES

ANSWERS TO PRAYER

SATURDAY, MARCH 23

*The Lord is my strength and my safe cover. My heart
trusts in Him, and I am helped. So my heart is full of joy.
I will thank Him with my song. The Lord is the strength
of His people. He is a safe place for His chosen one.*

PSALM 28:7–8 NLV

Lord, my unshakable joy comes from knowing You truly are my strength and cover,
my help and my hope. In any and all circumstances, You are my safe place. . . .

PRAYER REQUESTS

ANSWERS
TO PRAYER

PRAISES

SUNDAY, MARCH 24

Palm Sunday

The next day the great crowd that had come for the festival heard that Jesus was on his way to Jerusalem. They took palm branches and went out to meet him, shouting, "Hosanna!" "Blessed is he who comes in the name of the Lord!" "Blessed is the king of Israel!"

JOHN 12:12–13 NIV

You are the Savior, the Greatest One, Jesus! I'm excited for the day when I get to be with You and praise You forever in heaven....

PRAYER REQUESTS

PRAISES

ANSWERS TO PRAYER

MONDAY, MARCH 25

I have placed the Lord always in front of me. Because He is at my right hand, I will not be moved. And so my heart is glad. My soul is full of joy. My body also will rest without fear. For You will not give me over to the grave. And You will not allow Your Holy One to return to dust. You will show me the way of life. Being with You is to be full of joy. In Your right hand there is happiness forever.

PSALM 16:8–11 NLV

I lift this psalm up to You, Sovereign Lord! I praise You for this truth! . . .

PRAYER REQUESTS

ANSWERS TO PRAYER

PRAISES

TUESDAY, MARCH 26

May all who seek you rejoice and be glad in you! May those who love your salvation say evermore, "God is great!"
PSALM 70:4 ESV

I seek You, Lord, and I never want to stop! Fill me with gladness as I do. Help me to show others the purpose and joy and peace that come from seeking after You. I love Your salvation, and I proclaim to all who will listen that You are great! . . .

PRAYER REQUESTS

PRAISES

ANSWERS TO PRAYER

WEDNESDAY, MARCH 27

Our mouths were filled with laughter, our tongues with song of joy. Then it was said among the nations, "The LORD has done great things for them." The LORD has done great things for us, and we are filled with joy.

PSALM 126:2–3 NIV

If my joy is ever faltering, I simply need to think back over the many great things You have done for me, Lord. Every good gift in my life has ultimately come from You. Counting my blessings fills me with joy. . . .

PRAYER REQUESTS

ANSWERS
TO PRAYER

PRAISES

THURSDAY, MARCH 28

If we claim to be without sin, we deceive ourselves and the truth is not in us. If we confess our sins, he is faithful and just and will forgive us our sins and purify us from all unrighteousness.

1 John 1:8–9 NIV

Lord, I'm so grateful for the joy and relief that come from admitting my sins and asking for and receiving Your forgiveness. Thank You for Your grace and mercy! Please help me to never hold on to my sins and lie about them. I confess these sins to You. . . .

PRAYER REQUESTS

PRAISES

ANSWERS TO PRAYER

FRIDAY, MARCH 29

Good Friday

Weeping may last through the night,
but joy comes with the morning.

PSALM 30:5 NLT

There was surely much weeping by those who loved You on the day You suffered and died on the cross, Jesus. But joy was coming when You would rise again on the morning of the third day. When I am weeping over life's sorrows and fears, remind me that joy is coming. Your truth and love and hope comfort and sustain me until then. . . .

PRAYER REQUESTS

ANSWERS
TO PRAYER

PRAISES

SATURDAY, MARCH 30

Those who plant in tears will harvest with shouts of joy.
PSALM 126:5 NLT

On the day between Your death and resurrection, Jesus, little did Your followers know how true this scripture was. Though they were crying many tears, they would soon shout with joy to see You alive again. Let Your Word daily remind me that You will turn every one of my tears here on earth into perfect joy forever in heaven. . . .

PRAYER REQUESTS

PRAISES

ANSWERS TO PRAYER

SUNDAY, MARCH 31

Easter

The angel spoke to the women. "Don't be afraid!" he said. "I know you are looking for Jesus, who was crucified. He isn't here! He is risen from the dead, just as he said would happen. Come, see where his body was lying. And now, go quickly and tell his disciples that he has risen from the dead."

MATTHEW 28:5–7 NLT

Oh, Jesus, what incredible surprise and joy the women who were mourning You must have had at the angel's words! And then to see You risen! I have that joy today, too, trusting in You as my risen Savior. . . .

PRAYER REQUESTS

ANSWERS TO PRAYER

PRAISES

April

CULTIVATING PEACE

*You will keep in perfect peace all who trust
in you, all whose thoughts are fixed on you!*
Isaiah 26:3 NLT

SUNDAY	MONDAY	TUESDAY	WEDNESDAY	THURSDAY	FRIDAY	SATURDAY
	1	2	3	4	5	6
7	8	9	10	11	12	13
14	15	16	17	18	19	20
21	22 Passover Begins at Sundown	23	24	25	26	27
28	29	30				

What's the first step toward peace? Trust. Faith in the God who invites you to give Him all your burdens (Psalm 55:22). Next is having confidence that He has everything—from the big things to the small—under control. Ask Him to shower peace in every area of your life, and He will deliver.

MONDAY, APRIL 1

"I have told you these things, so that in me you may
have peace. In this world you will have trouble.
But take heart! I have overcome the world."

JOHN 16:33 NIV

Jesus, there is so much turmoil—both in the world and in my own life—that I know peace can only come from You. So I'm humbly asking for Your peace. Help me to take heart, knowing that You have everything that concerns me—and more—under control. I trust You, my Savior and Lord. . . .

PRAYER REQUESTS

ANSWERS TO PRAYER

PRAISES

TUESDAY, APRIL 2

Do not conform to the pattern of this world, but be transformed by the renewing of your mind. Then you will be able to test and approve what God's will is—his good, pleasing and perfect will.
ROMANS 12:2 NIV

Even when all is quiet, Father, I can't seem to hush my anxious mind. So today I ask You to be present in my thoughts. Renew and refresh my inner dialogue and help me to think Your thoughts so I can know and understand You better. . . .

PRAYER REQUESTS

PRAISES

ANSWERS TO PRAYER

WEDNESDAY, APRIL 3

Now may the Lord of peace Himself
give you peace always by all means.
2 Thessalonians 3:16 SKJV

I take comfort in the fact that scripture names You the Lord of peace, Father. I surrender the parts of my life that aren't peaceful, and I ask You to envelop them with Your care, comfort, and provision. When I stubbornly hold on to strife, remind me that Your way is better. No matter what the day brings, help me rest in You. . . .

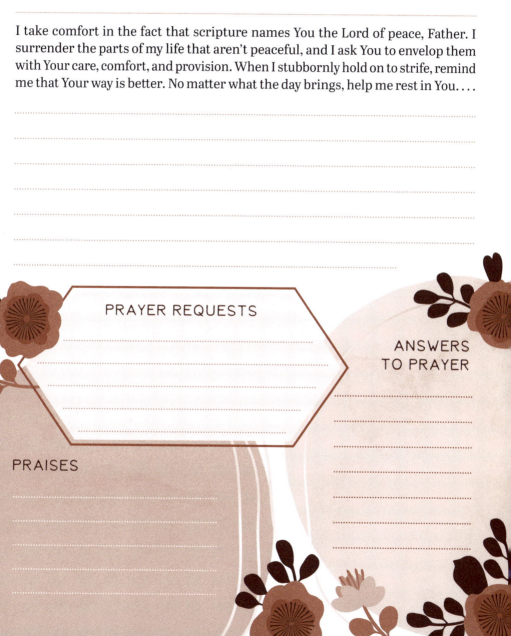

PRAYER REQUESTS

ANSWERS TO PRAYER

PRAISES

THURSDAY, APRIL 4

"Blessed are the peacemakers, for they shall be called the children of God."

MATTHEW 5:9 SKJV

Jesus, show me how to bring peace to my world—in my own home and community. Please give me opportunities where I can spread Your peace in my words and actions. Focus my thoughts on Your greatest commands—love God and love others—so that others can see and experience Your goodness. As Your child, Father, I want to display Your character everywhere I go. . . .

PRAYER REQUESTS

PRAISES

ANSWERS TO PRAYER

FRIDAY, APRIL 5

Don't worry about anything; instead, pray about everything.
Tell God what you need, and thank him for all he has done.

PHILIPPIANS 4:6 NLT

Father, Your Word says in 1 Peter 5:7 that You'll carry my burdens. So today I lay down my worries at Your feet. Please hold them out of my reach so I'm not tempted to take them back. Instead of worrying, I will pray. Thank You for listening to my concerns and for caring for me so well. . . .

PRAYER REQUESTS

ANSWERS
TO PRAYER

PRAISES

SATURDAY, APRIL 6

"Peace I leave with you. My peace I give to you. I do not give peace to you as the world gives. Do not let your hearts be troubled or afraid."
JOHN 14:27 NLV

Jesus, my heart seems so prone to fear, but the only way to keep my anxious feelings away is to fill my heart with Your perfect peace. Today, give me an extra portion of Your peace. Please make Your Spirit come alive in me with the comfort of Your love and goodness. . . .

PRAYER REQUESTS

PRAISES

ANSWERS TO PRAYER

SUNDAY, APRIL 7

Do all that you can to live in peace with everyone.
ROMANS 12:18 NLT

Father, I can live peacefully with many people, but the ones who push my buttons. . . well, that's another story. When I am struggling with a less-than-peaceful attitude toward others, remind me that You love them unconditionally and that they are created in Your image. Help me to understand them in a new way and see the benefits of pursuing peace. With Your help, I will do all that I can to live in peace. . . .

PRAYER REQUESTS

ANSWERS
TO PRAYER

PRAISES

MONDAY, APRIL 8

Let the peace that comes from Christ rule in
your hearts. For as members of one body you are
called to live in peace. And always be thankful.
COLOSSIANS 3:15 NLT

Jesus, thank You for the part I play in Your church and for the family of God I have found there. We are imperfect, but we strive to love You and love each other. Help us to lay aside our pride and be unified in our goal to share You with the world. . . .

PRAYER REQUESTS

PRAISES

ANSWERS TO PRAYER

TUESDAY, APRIL 9

In peace I will lie down and sleep, for you alone, LORD, make me dwell in safety.

PSALM 4:8 NIV

You are my safe keeper, Lord. For all the times You have quieted my heart, given me hope for the future, and allowed me to be still in Your presence, thank You. Keep my body, mind, heart, and soul safe in Your arms. Shield me from harm today, Father, and as the day fades into night, grant me peaceful sleep. . . .

PRAYER REQUESTS

ANSWERS TO PRAYER

PRAISES

WEDNESDAY, APRIL 10

The mind governed by the Spirit is life and peace.
ROMANS 8:6 NIV

Holy Spirit, You are the key to my inner peace. When my mind is filled with worries, anxious thoughts, fears, and frustrations, that tells me I have taken back control from You. So I surrender my mind to Your good guidance. Help me hear Your voice. Lead me to an inner life that is centered on the things of God—a life that overflows with peace and love that others can experience too. . . .

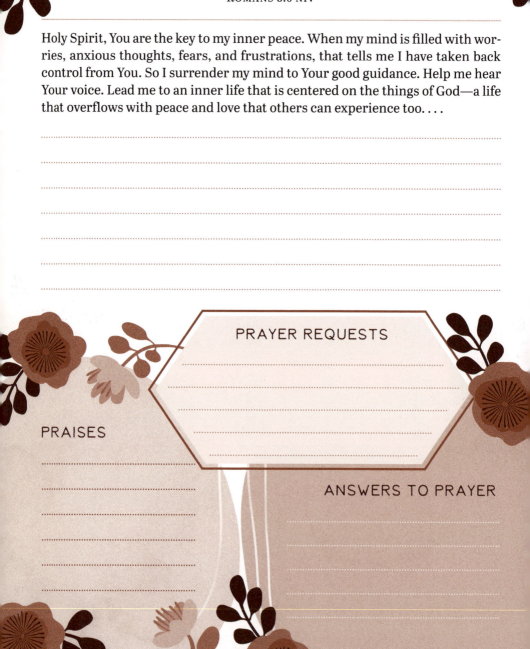

PRAYER REQUESTS

PRAISES

ANSWERS TO PRAYER

THURSDAY, APRIL 11

Search for peace, and work to maintain it.
1 PETER 3:11 NLT

God, make me an active peacemaker who seeks out Your peace. Give me the wisdom to build strong relationships with friends, family, coworkers, and acquaintances. Help me anticipate problems and proactively deal with them before they happen. When conflict arises, help me to be part of the solution to restore calm wholeness. I want to be a source of life and light to everyone around me. . . .

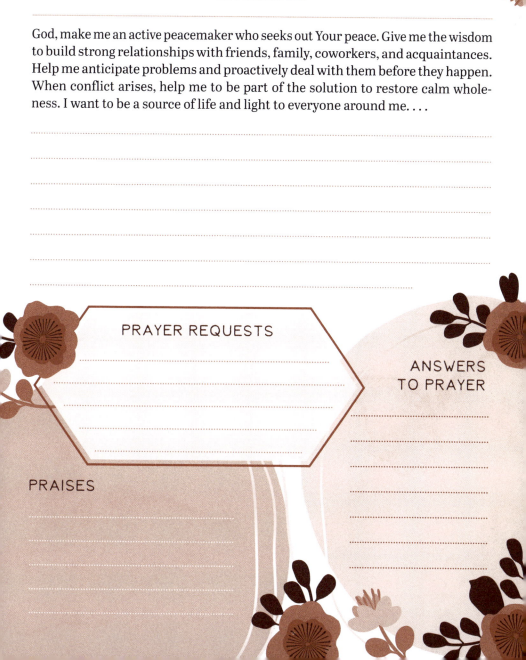

PRAYER REQUESTS

ANSWERS TO PRAYER

PRAISES

FRIDAY, APRIL 12

God is not a God of disorder but of peace.
1 CORINTHIANS 14:33 NIV

Thank You, Father, for being the embodiment of peace. When I run to You, I don't have to worry that I will have a chaotic encounter. You are the rock I can anchor to. When I am in turmoil, You are the balm that soothes my heart and calms the storm in my mind. When I am frightened, Your solid arms protect me and Your steady hand guides me. . . .

PRAYER REQUESTS

PRAISES

ANSWERS TO PRAYER

SATURDAY, APRIL 13

The peace of God is much greater than the human mind can understand. This peace will keep your hearts and minds through Christ Jesus.
PHILIPPIANS 4:7 NLV

Wrap me in the mystery of Your peace, Father God. I will never understand it fully, but I do understand how Your peace makes me feel: loved, protected, calm, and hopeful. Help me to share the assurance of Your peace in the turmoil I see around me. I need more of You and less of the world's chaos, Father. . . .

PRAYER REQUESTS

ANSWERS TO PRAYER

PRAISES

SUNDAY, APRIL 14

When people's lives please the LORD,
even their enemies are at peace with them.
PROVERBS 16:7 NLT

I dedicate today to Your pleasure, Lord God. Make my life an example of unending peace that only You can provide. Give me the wisdom to live peacefully with everyone—even people I don't agree with. With help from Your Spirit living inside me, I will extend Your love in all circumstances, and I know You will bless me because of it. . . .

PRAYER REQUESTS

PRAISES

ANSWERS TO PRAYER

MONDAY, APRIL 15

*Work for the things that make peace and help
each other become stronger Christians.*
ROMANS 14:19 NLV

God, please give us unity within Your church. We are individuals who love You, and sometimes our own opinions and selfishness get in the way of the peace that You offer us. Forgive me when I add to that discord. Help me to encourage my brothers and sisters in their faith journeys, instead, so that we can all grow stronger together in You. . . .

PRAYER REQUESTS

ANSWERS
TO PRAYER

PRAISES

TUESDAY, APRIL 16

Be joyful. Grow to maturity. Encourage each other. Live in harmony and peace. Then the God of love and peace will be with you.
2 CORINTHIANS 13:11 NLT

Father, thank You for offering Your children a life that is so full and overflowing with goodness. Today, I will find joy in the details of life. Help me build up the people around me and promote harmony. I can't do these things by myself, Lord. I need more of You in every way. . . .

PRAYER REQUESTS

PRAISES

ANSWERS TO PRAYER

WEDNESDAY, APRIL 17

"Though the mountains be shaken and the hills be removed,
yet my unfailing love for you will not be shaken nor my covenant
of peace be removed," says the Lord, who has compassion on you.

Isaiah 54:10 niv

Compassionate Father, thank You for loving me unconditionally and without stipulations. The bigness of Your love overwhelms me when I try to understand it. But the truth is that Your love gives me a deep, lasting peace and comfort no matter what is going on around me. . . .

PRAYER REQUESTS

ANSWERS
TO PRAYER

PRAISES

THURSDAY, APRIL 18

The wisdom from above is first of all pure. It is also peace loving, gentle at all times, and willing to yield to others. It is full of mercy and the fruit of good deeds. It shows no favoritism and is always sincere.

JAMES 3:17 NLT

God, please give me more of Your wisdom so that when life throws obstacles my way, I can respond with peaceful, gentle words and actions. When I feel conflict arise with another person, give me patience and genuine care for them. . . .

PRAYER REQUESTS

PRAISES

ANSWERS TO PRAYER

FRIDAY, APRIL 19

Don't repay evil for evil. Don't retaliate with insults when people insult you. Instead, pay them back with a blessing. That is what God has called you to do, and he will grant you his blessing.

1 Peter 3:9 NLT

I need Your help when I feel attacked, Lord. Because the truth is, when someone hurts me, I want to hurt them even more. Instead, help me to learn from Your example. You bless me even when I make mistakes. Help me to offer the same grace to others. . . .

PRAYER REQUESTS

ANSWERS TO PRAYER

PRAISES

SATURDAY, APRIL 20

*He was hurt for our wrong-doing. He was crushed
for our sins. He was punished so we would have
peace. He was beaten so we would be healed.*

ISAIAH 53:5 NLV

Jesus, You willingly allowed Yourself to be humiliated and mutilated and killed on a cross for my healing and peace. I am so thankful for the wholeness I experience because of the brokenness You endured. Thank You for being the restorative Savior of my soul for now and all eternity. . . .

PRAYER REQUESTS

PRAISES

ANSWERS TO PRAYER

SUNDAY, APRIL 21

Mercy, peace and love be yours in abundance.
JUDE 2 NIV

Father, I need more mercy in my life. Thank You for Your daily little graces that remind me of Your forgiveness and compassion. Help me offer the same mercy to others. Please be in the details—both big and small—of my day. And when problems arise, give me the ability to look past them and shower peace in any situation. Help me be the goodness I want to see in the world. . . .

PRAYER REQUESTS

ANSWERS TO PRAYER

PRAISES

MONDAY, APRIL 22

Passover Begins at Sundown

*How beautiful on the mountains are the feet of the messenger
who brings good news, the good news of peace and salvation.*

ISAIAH 52:7 NLT

I have a life-giving message in my heart, Father—the good news of Your saving love
and gift of grace! Give me opportunities to share that message with people who
need more peace and more assurance of Your good plans for them. Give me Your
words to speak life into my relationships, home, and work. . . .

PRAYER REQUESTS

PRAISES

ANSWERS TO PRAYER

TUESDAY, APRIL 23

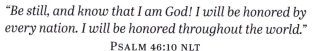

"Be still, and know that I am God! I will be honored by every nation. I will be honored throughout the world."
PSALM 46:10 NLT

Almighty God, there are storms inside me and turmoil all around me. Instead of trying to fix it all, first I will *be still*. I will *listen* for Your voice. And I will *know* on the deepest soul level that You are God. You are in charge. You are in control. And You are a good, good Father. . . .

PRAYER REQUESTS

ANSWERS TO PRAYER

PRAISES

WEDNESDAY, APRIL 24

"May the Lord show favor toward you, and give you peace."
NUMBERS 6:26 NLV

Father, I am not deserving of Your favor, yet You choose to bless me. Thank You for protecting me and my loved ones. Thank You for Your gifts of mercy and compassion every day. Thank You for the gift of Your Son, whose sacrifice makes me worthy of being called Your daughter. Thank You for the hope I have in You for today, tomorrow, and eternity. . . .

PRAYER REQUESTS

PRAISES

ANSWERS TO PRAYER

THURSDAY, APRIL 25

Jesus said, "Come to me, all of you who are weary and carry heavy burdens, and I will give you rest."
MATTHEW 11:28 NLT

Some days I am physically, mentally, and spiritually tired, Lord. When my gas tank is empty, fill me up with Your Spirit. Jesus, I am throwing my burdens at Your feet because I know You'll sort through the things that weigh me down and You'll carry what needs to come along on the journey. Thank You for the gift of rest. . . .

PRAYER REQUESTS

ANSWERS TO PRAYER

PRAISES

FRIDAY, APRIL 26

*"You will go out with joy, and be led out in peace. The mountains
and the hills will break out into sounds of joy before you.
And all the trees of the field will clap their hands."*
ISAIAH 55:12 NLV

God, lead me in peace today. When I'm centered in Your will, that's when I experience true joy that overflows from my heart. Reveal Yourself in Your creation, and help me to know that everything is as it should be because You are in control. . . .

PRAYER REQUESTS

PRAISES

ANSWERS TO PRAYER

SATURDAY, APRIL 27

No discipline is enjoyable while it is happening—
it's painful! But afterward there will be a peaceful harvest
of right living for those who are trained in this way.
HEBREWS 12:11 NLT

I know You are my loving Father, but it's still hard to receive discipline from You, Lord. Today, I choose to be thankful through the pain of discipline. I will endure because I know You are leading me to a peaceful future that's more deeply rooted in Your love. . . .

PRAYER REQUESTS

ANSWERS TO PRAYER

PRAISES

SUNDAY, APRIL 28

For Christ himself has brought peace to us. He united Jews and Gentiles into one people when, in his own body on the cross, he broke down the wall of hostility that separated us.

EPHESIANS 2:14 NLT

Jesus, when I am tempted to focus on the differences between myself and other Christians, remind me that Your death unifies us all in Your kingdom. We are Your beloved siblings, and we all call upon the same Father God. Unite us in the love we have for You and for each other. . . .

PRAYER REQUESTS

PRAISES

ANSWERS TO PRAYER

MONDAY, APRIL 29

Unfailing love and truth have met together.
Righteousness and peace have kissed!
PSALM 85:10 NLT

Father, when I let Your goodness reign over my life, I am astounded at the goodness that surrounds me. Unfailing love. Truth. Righteous peace. Hope and an unwavering sense of wholeness envelop me and sustain me even when I'm going through difficult times. Thank You for being my constant source of light and life. Help me direct others to the beacon of Your love. . . .

PRAYER REQUESTS

ANSWERS
TO PRAYER

PRAISES

TUESDAY, APRIL 30

If you lie down, you will not be afraid;
when you lie down, your sleep will be sweet.
PROVERBS 3:24 ESV

I long for sweet sleep, Lord. When I let my anxious thoughts control my mind at night, my sleep is anything but sweet. Take away my fears, Father. I give You my concerns about tomorrow, and I will not worry my sleep away. With my heart and mind centered on You, I will experience true, restorative rest that will prepare me to follow You when I rise tomorrow. . . .

PRAYER REQUESTS

PRAISES

ANSWERS TO PRAYER

May
LEARNING PATIENCE

Be still in the presence of the LORD,
and wait patiently for him to act.

PSALM 37:7 NLT

SUNDAY	MONDAY	TUESDAY	WEDNESDAY	THURSDAY	FRIDAY	SATURDAY
			1	2 National Day of Prayer	3	4
5	6	7	8	9	10	11
12 Mother's Day	13	14	15	16	17	18
19	20	21	22	23	24	25
26	27 Memorial Day	28	29	30	31	

It's nice when God's timing matches exactly what we hope for, but that's not always the case. Often we find ourselves waiting on God, and those waiting times are *hard*. Yet, our Father calls us to have patience—something He will help us continually learn and mature in if we let Him.

WEDNESDAY, MAY 1

In everything we do, we show that we are true ministers of God. We patiently endure troubles and hardships and calamities of every kind. . . . We prove ourselves by our purity, our understanding, our patience, our kindness, by the Holy Spirit within us, and by our sincere love. We faithfully preach the truth. God's power is working in us.

2 Corinthians 6:4, 6–7 nlt

Lord, I want this scripture to be true of me! Please let Your power work in me. . . .

PRAYER REQUESTS

PRAISES

ANSWERS TO PRAYER

THURSDAY, MAY 2

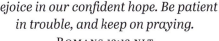
National Day of Prayer

*Rejoice in our confident hope. Be patient
in trouble, and keep on praying.*

ROMANS 12:12 NLT

With so many needs and troubles in the world, Lord, it's hard to know where to begin praying for them. Not to mention the needs and troubles in my own life and in the lives of my loved ones. But through them all, I choose to rejoice in You—my confident hope—with patience and trust, and I will keep on praying. . . .

PRAYER REQUESTS

ANSWERS TO PRAYER

PRAISES

FRIDAY, MAY 3

*When God made a promise to Abraham, He made that
promise in His own name because no one was greater.
He said, "I will make you happy in so many ways. For sure,
I will give you many children." Abraham was willing to
wait and God gave to him what He had promised.*

HEBREWS 6:13–15 NLV

Heavenly Father, let me learn from Abraham's example. I want to always be willing
to wait on You. I trust You will fulfill Your promises. I trust You will bless me in
Your perfect timing. . . .

PRAYER REQUESTS

PRAISES

ANSWERS TO PRAYER

SATURDAY, MAY 4

I would have lost strength, but I believed I would see the goodness of the LORD in the land of the living. Wait on the LORD. Be of good courage, and He shall strengthen your heart. Wait, I say, on the LORD.
PSALM 27:13–14 SKJV

I too will lose strength unless I keep faith in You, Lord! I will wait patiently on You with courage. I believe that You will strengthen me and that I will see Your goodness. . . .

PRAYER REQUESTS

ANSWERS TO PRAYER

PRAISES

SUNDAY, MAY 5

We, too, wait with eager hope for the day when God will give us our full rights as his adopted children, including the new bodies he has promised us. We were given this hope when we were saved. (If we already have something, we don't need to hope for it. But if we look forward to something we don't yet have, we must wait patiently and confidently.)

ROMANS 8:23–25 NLT

Some days, I feel so weary of this crazy world, Lord. But I will trust You patiently with eager hope. I know You will keep all Your promises. . . .

PRAYER REQUESTS

PRAISES

ANSWERS TO PRAYER

MONDAY, MAY 6

*So the Lord wants to show you kindness. He waits on high to
have loving-pity on you. For the Lord is a God of what is right
and fair. And good will come to all those who hope in Him.*

ISAIAH 30:18 NLV

Lord God, thank You for always being right and fair. You are the one true God of justice. I believe good will come to me as I hope in You and wait patiently for Your perfect timing in all things. . . .

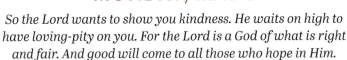

PRAYER REQUESTS

ANSWERS
TO PRAYER

PRAISES

*When you, a mere human being, pass judgment on them
and yet do the same things, do you think you will escape
God's judgment? Or do you show contempt for the riches of
his kindness, forbearance and patience, not realizing that
God's kindness is intended to lead you to repentance?*

ROMANS 2:3–4 NIV

Heavenly Father, please forgive me for passing judgment on others when instead I need to be examining my own attitudes and actions. You have been so patient and gracious with me, and I want to extend patience and grace to others. . . .

PRAYER REQUESTS

PRAISES

ANSWERS TO PRAYER

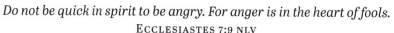

WEDNESDAY, MAY 8

Do not be quick in spirit to be angry. For anger is in the heart of fools.
ECCLESIASTES 7:9 NLV

Father, please forgive me for the times when I have been far too quick to get angry. Please help me to be calm and steady in the midst of upsetting circumstances. It's so easy to sin in these times, but I want to have patience and self-control and to deal with the problem in wise ways, the ways You want me to. . . .

PRAYER REQUESTS

ANSWERS TO PRAYER

PRAISES

THURSDAY, MAY 9

I did not give up waiting for the Lord. And He turned to me and heard my cry. He brought me up out of the hole of danger, out of the mud and clay. He set my feet on a rock, making my feet sure. He put a new song in my mouth, a song of praise to our God.

PSALM 40:1–3 NLV

Lord, even when life is so hard, I don't ever want to give up waiting on You. I trust that when I wait patiently, I will experience Your answer and blessing. . . .

PRAYER REQUESTS

PRAISES

ANSWERS TO PRAYER

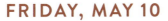

FRIDAY, MAY 10

God is not unjust; he will not forget your work and the love you have shown him as you have helped his people and continue to help them. We want each of you to show this same diligence to the very end, so that what you hope for may be fully realized. We do not want you to become lazy, but to imitate those who through faith and patience inherit what has been promised.

HEBREWS 6:10–12 NIV

God, thank You that You see my good work and want to bless me. Please help me to never grow lazy in helping others. Give me the faith and patience I need to keep going. . . .

PRAYER REQUESTS

ANSWERS TO PRAYER

PRAISES

SATURDAY, MAY 11

For God is pleased when, conscious of his will, you patiently endure unjust treatment. Of course, you get no credit for being patient if you are beaten for doing wrong. But if you suffer for doing good and endure it patiently, God is pleased with you. For God called you to do good, even if it means suffering, just as Christ suffered for you. He is your example, and you must follow in his steps.

1 Peter 2:19–21 NLT

Jesus, You are my example. Please hold me close and help me to patiently endure suffering as I follow in Your steps. . . .

PRAYER REQUESTS

PRAISES

ANSWERS TO PRAYER

SUNDAY, MAY 12
Mother's Day

Love is patient, love is kind. It does not envy, it does not boast, it is not proud. It does not dishonor others, it is not self-seeking, it is not easily angered, it keeps no record of wrongs. Love does not delight in evil but rejoices with the truth. It always protects, always trusts, always hopes, always perseveres. Love never fails.

1 CORINTHIANS 13:4–8 NIV

Lord, thank You for the ways so many good mothers are so patient and kind—true examples of real love. . . .

PRAYER REQUESTS

ANSWERS TO PRAYER

PRAISES

MONDAY, MAY 13

We also pray that you will be strengthened with all his glorious power so you will have all the endurance and patience you need. May you be filled with joy, always thanking the Father. He has enabled you to share in the inheritance that belongs to his people, who live in the light. For he has rescued us from the kingdom of darkness and transferred us into the Kingdom of his dear Son, who purchased our freedom and forgave our sins.
COLOSSIANS 1:11–14 NLT

Father, please strengthen me with Your glorious power so that I will have all the endurance and patience I need. . . .

PRAYER REQUESTS

PRAISES

ANSWERS TO PRAYER

TUESDAY, MAY 14

A soft answer turns away wrath, but a harsh word stirs up anger.
PROVERBS 15:1 ESV

I confess that when I'm feeling impatient, I often speak too harshly in anger and frustration. Please forgive me, Lord. Help me to choose soft, loving words toward others, even in the midst of frustration, anger, and impatience. Remind me that angry words just escalate things, but soft responses help defuse a stressful situation....

PRAYER REQUESTS

ANSWERS TO PRAYER

PRAISES

WEDNESDAY, MAY 15

Just as we share abundantly in the sufferings of Christ,
so also our comfort abounds through Christ. If we are
distressed, it is for your comfort and salvation; if we are
comforted, it is for your comfort, which produces in you
patient endurance of the same sufferings we suffer.

2 CORINTHIANS 1:5–6 NIV

Lord, please help me to be patient and positive in the midst of suffering. I trust You will draw me close and comfort me, and in turn I can share that comfort with others. . . .

PRAYER REQUESTS

PRAISES

ANSWERS TO PRAYER

THURSDAY, MAY 16

*But they who wait for the LORD shall renew their strength;
they shall mount up with wings like eagles; they shall run
and not be weary; they shall walk and not faint.*
ISAIAH 40:31 ESV

In Your perfect timing, Lord, I trust I will have strength to overcome. I will fly
with victory and triumph over the trials I am facing. . . .

PRAYER REQUESTS

ANSWERS TO PRAYER

PRAISES

FRIDAY, MAY 17

Here is a trustworthy saying that deserves full acceptance: Christ Jesus came into the world to save sinners—of whom I am the worst. But for that very reason I was shown mercy so that in me, the worst of sinners, Christ Jesus might display his immense patience as an example for those who would believe in him and receive eternal life.

1 TIMOTHY 1:15–16 NIV

You are the perfect example of patience and mercy, Jesus. Thank You for saving me from my sin. I want to be more and more like You. . . .

PRAYER REQUESTS

PRAISES

ANSWERS TO PRAYER

SATURDAY, MAY 18

"And the seeds that fell on the good soil represent honest, good-hearted people who hear God's word, cling to it, and patiently produce a huge harvest."

LUKE 8:15 NLT

God, help me to remember the parable of the seeds and soils. I want to hear Your Word, cling to it, and patiently produce a huge harvest. . . .

PRAYER REQUESTS

ANSWERS TO PRAYER

PRAISES

SUNDAY, MAY 19

Live in peace with each other. And we urge you, brothers and sisters, warn those who are idle and disruptive, encourage the disheartened, help the weak, be patient with everyone. Make sure that nobody pays back wrong for wrong, but always strive to do what is good for each other and for everyone else.

1 Thessalonians 5:13–15 NIV

Lord, please help me to have the love and patience and right attitudes I should have to live in good relationship with the people You have brought into my life....

PRAYER REQUESTS

PRAISES

ANSWERS TO PRAYER

MONDAY, MAY 20

So then, dear friends, since you are looking forward to this, make every effort to be found spotless, blameless and at peace with him. Bear in mind that our Lord's patience means salvation, just as our dear brother Paul also wrote you with the wisdom that God gave him.

2 PETER 3:14–15 NIV

Lord, remind me that You are patient on purpose, and I should be too. As I wait for Your timing, please help me to do my best to be found spotless, blameless, and at peace with You. . . .

PRAYER REQUESTS

ANSWERS TO PRAYER

PRAISES

TUESDAY, MAY 21

But Moses told the people, "Don't be afraid. Just stand still and watch the LORD rescue you today. The Egyptians you see today will never be seen again. The LORD himself will fight for you. Just stay calm."

EXODUS 14:13–14 NLT

Lord, help me to learn from this example. Sometimes I just need to be still, wait patiently, and let You do all the work as You fight for me and rescue me from those working against me. Please guide me daily in knowing when to act and when to be still. . . .

PRAYER REQUESTS

PRAISES

ANSWERS TO PRAYER

WEDNESDAY, MAY 22

A person's wisdom yields patience;
it is to one's glory to overlook an offense.
PROVERBS 19:11 NIV

Father, please mature me with wisdom, and with that wisdom help me to have more patience. Remind me that it's a blessing to give others extra grace for mistakes and offenses, just like I so often need extra grace for my mistakes and offenses. . . .

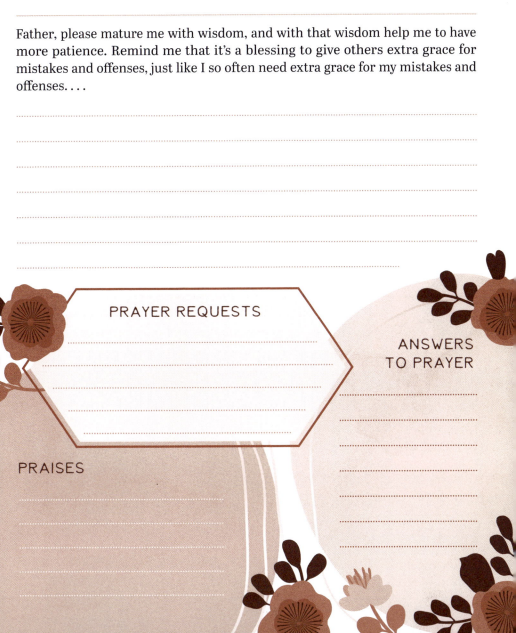

PRAYER REQUESTS

ANSWERS
TO PRAYER

PRAISES

THURSDAY, MAY 23

Let us not become weary in doing good, for at the proper time we will reap a harvest if we do not give up. Therefore, as we have opportunity, let us do good to all people, especially to those who belong to the family of believers.

GALATIANS 6:9–10 NIV

With energy that comes from You, Lord, please help me not to grow weary in doing good. I don't want to give up on the plans You have for me to share Your love with others. . . .

PRAYER REQUESTS

PRAISES

ANSWERS TO PRAYER

FRIDAY, MAY 24

A hot-tempered person starts fights;
a cool-tempered person stops them.
PROVERBS 15:18 NLT

I admit I'm sometimes hot-tempered, Father. I can get angry too easily and start unnecessary conflict. Certain situations and certain people just push my buttons. Please forgive me and help me ask forgiveness from those I've hurt. Help me to have more patience. Keep my temper calm, cool, and collected. . . .

PRAYER REQUESTS

ANSWERS TO PRAYER

PRAISES

SATURDAY, MAY 25

He will render to each one according to his works:
to those who by patience in well-doing seek for glory
and honor and immortality, he will give eternal life;
but for those who are self-seeking and do not obey the truth,
but obey unrighteousness, there will be wrath and fury.
ROMANS 2:6–8 ESV

Lord, I want to constantly have patience to do good things for Your glory and not for my own selfish interests. Help me to lovingly and tirelessly do the good works You have planned for me. . . .

PRAYER REQUESTS

PRAISES

ANSWERS TO PRAYER

SUNDAY, MAY 26

May God, who gives this patience and encouragement, help you live in complete harmony with each other, as is fitting for followers of Christ Jesus. Then all of you can join together with one voice, giving praise and glory to God, the Father of our Lord Jesus Christ.
ROMANS 15:5–6 NLT

God, please generously give me Your patience and encouragement to help me live in harmony with fellow followers of Jesus. Let us bring praise and glory to You with our love and care for each other! . . .

PRAYER REQUESTS

ANSWERS TO PRAYER

PRAISES

MONDAY, MAY 27

Memorial Day

For examples of patience in suffering, dear brothers and sisters, look at the prophets who spoke in the name of the Lord. We give great honor to those who endure under suffering. For instance, you know about Job, a man of great endurance. You can see how the Lord was kind to him at the end, for the Lord is full of tenderness and mercy.

JAMES 5:10–11 NLT

Lord, I want to keep looking to Your Word and the prophets who spoke in Your name for examples and inspiration and encouragement. . . .

PRAYER REQUESTS

PRAISES

ANSWERS TO PRAYER

TUESDAY, MAY 28

"For I know the plans I have for you, declares the LORD,
plans for welfare and not for evil, to give you a future and a hope."
JEREMIAH 29:11 ESV

I believe You have good plans for Your people, Lord, and that includes me. Sometimes I'm just so impatient waiting and wanting to know what those plans are right here, right now. Help me not want to rush You, Lord. . . .

PRAYER REQUESTS

PRAISES

ANSWERS TO PRAYER

WEDNESDAY, MAY 29

*Do not be anxious about anything, but in everything
by prayer and supplication with thanksgiving
let your requests be made known to God.*
PHILIPPIANS 4:6 ESV

Heavenly Father, in my times of waiting on You, I don't want to be anxious. Help me to give those fears and worries to You and to focus on prayer, supplication, and thanksgiving instead! Help me to use my wait times wisely. . . .

PRAYER REQUESTS

PRAISES

ANSWERS TO PRAYER

THURSDAY, MAY 30

Be patient, then, brothers and sisters, until the Lord's coming.
See how the farmer waits for the land to yield its valuable crop,
patiently waiting for the autumn and spring rains. You too, be
patient and stand firm, because the Lord's coming is near.
JAMES 5:7–8 NIV

I'm thankful Your coming is near, Lord! We need You! Help me to stand firm as I wait for You patiently while doing the good things You have planned for me to help build Your kingdom. . . .

PRAYER REQUESTS

ANSWERS
TO PRAYER

PRAISES

FRIDAY, MAY 31

But you must not forget this one thing, dear friends: A day is like a thousand years to the Lord, and a thousand years is like a day. The Lord isn't really being slow about his promise, as some people think. No, he is being patient for your sake. He does not want anyone to be destroyed, but wants everyone to repent.

2 PETER 3:8–9 NLT

Lord, remind me that Your timing is far beyond my comprehension and that You are compassionate toward all people, wanting them to come to salvation in You. . . .

PRAYER REQUESTS

PRAISES

ANSWERS TO PRAYER

June

PRACTICING KINDNESS

You must be kind to each other. Think of the other person. Forgive other people just as God forgave you.
EPHESIANS 4:32 NLV

SUNDAY	MONDAY	TUESDAY	WEDNESDAY	THURSDAY	FRIDAY	SATURDAY
						1
2	3	4	5	6	7	8
9	10	11	12	13	14 Flag Day	15
16	17	18	19	20 First Day of Summer	21	22
Father's Day 23 30	24	25	26	27	28	29

There are situations where kindness comes easy. But the real challenge of God's command to be kind comes when it's hard to be kind. Remember the kindness that has been shown to you in your life. Ask God to help you, because we serve a powerful God who is also kind.

SATURDAY, JUNE 1

*"Love your enemies, and do good, and lend, hoping
for nothing back. And your reward shall be great,
and you shall be the children of the Highest."*
LUKE 6:35 SKJV

God, all I have is Yours. You provide me with all I need and more. I want to use those finances and physical things to be a blessing to others. Show me opportunities to give lavishly and with a joyful heart, knowing that You will be glorified. Thank You for being such a generous God. . . .

PRAYER REQUESTS

PRAISES

ANSWERS TO PRAYER

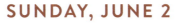

SUNDAY, JUNE 2

Your kindness will reward you, but your cruelty will destroy you.
PROVERBS 11:17 NLT

When showing kindness seems inconvenient or like too much work, Jesus, remind me that the reward is much greater than the effort. I know from my own experience that both the person showing kindness and the person receiving kindness benefit from it. I know I will be blessed when I take the time to be kind. Thank You for Your unending kindness to me, my Lord and Savior. . . .

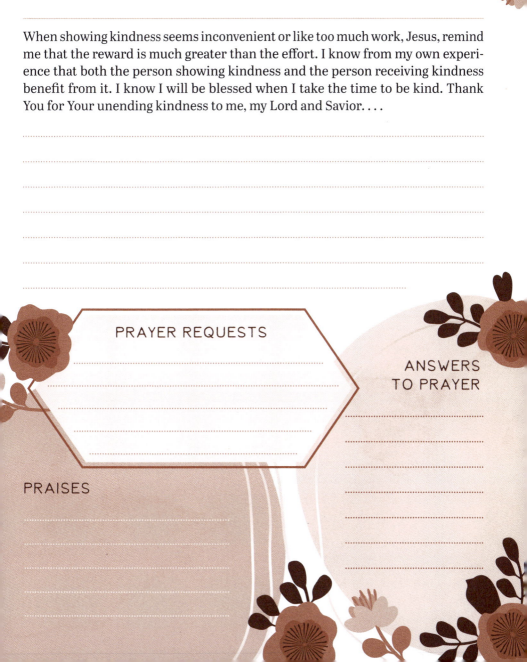

PRAYER REQUESTS

ANSWERS
TO PRAYER

PRAISES

MONDAY, JUNE 3

Therefore, as God's chosen people, holy and dearly loved, clothe yourselves with compassion, kindness, humility, gentleness and patience.
COLOSSIANS 3:12 NIV

Just as I choose the clothes I wear every day, Lord, I choose to put on Your attributes of compassion, kindness, humility, gentleness, and patience. Make them part of my very soul so they will be the focus of every interaction, every conversation, every thought, and every moment of my day. I want to be more like You, God. . . .

PRAYER REQUESTS

PRAISES

ANSWERS TO PRAYER

TUESDAY, JUNE 4

*If you help the poor, you are lending
to the LORD—and he will repay you!*
PROVERBS 19:17 NLT

I see so many needs around me, Father. Children who are hungry, families who need help through a tough time, people displaced by natural disasters. Those needs are great, but You are greater. You have given me a bounty of resources—more than I deserve—so please show me where, how, and who to help first. Please bless that gift and be glorified. . . .

PRAYER REQUESTS

ANSWERS TO PRAYER

PRAISES

WEDNESDAY, JUNE 5

*So then, as we have opportunity, let us do good to everyone,
and especially to those who are of the household of faith.*
GALATIANS 6:10 ESV

When I am on the receiving end of some unexpected kindness, Lord, I am always a little surprised. But it's the best kind of surprise. Encouragement, help, a little pick-me-up seems to come at the right time. Show me opportunities to do the same for others today, Father. My eyes and ears are open. . . .

PRAYER REQUESTS

PRAISES

ANSWERS TO PRAYER

THURSDAY, JUNE 6

*Don't be selfish; don't try to impress others. Be humble,
thinking of others as better than yourselves.*
PHILIPPIANS 2:3 NLT

When I am tempted to look down on someone else, check my heart, God. You have created each person with purpose, with Your unending love, and the worthiness to be called Your child. Jesus gave up His life for that person in the same way He did for me. Take away my selfishness, and help me see them through Your eyes. . . .

PRAYER REQUESTS

ANSWERS TO PRAYER

PRAISES

FRIDAY, JUNE 7

Love does not give up. Love is kind. Love is not jealous.
Love does not put itself up as being important. Love has no pride.

1 CORINTHIANS 13:4 NLV

Your love inhabits all the traits I want more of, God. Today, I will be kind in word, deed, and attitude. I will celebrate with others. And I will strive to think of others before I think of myself. Father, You know this will be hard to do, so I'm asking for Your help. . . .

PRAYER REQUESTS

PRAISES

ANSWERS TO PRAYER

SATURDAY, JUNE 8

If someone has enough money to live well and sees a brother or sister in need but shows no compassion— how can God's love be in that person?

1 John 3:17 nlt

Loving Father, You show me so much compassion. Your mercies are new every day (and I need them every day!). But sometimes I struggle to show compassion to others I see in need. Prod my heart to give without reservation when opportunities arise. I will display Your love so others see You more. . . .

PRAYER REQUESTS

ANSWERS TO PRAYER

PRAISES

SUNDAY, JUNE 9

*The Lord has told you what is good, and this
is what he requires of you: to do what is right,
to love mercy, and to walk humbly with your God.*
MICAH 6:8 NLT

I know injustice breaks Your heart, Holy Spirit. I'm asking You to give me the
courage to stand up and do what's right. Give me the wisdom to know what is
right in tough situations, and give me even more wisdom to do and say all things
with humility. . . .

PRAYER REQUESTS

PRAISES

ANSWERS TO PRAYER

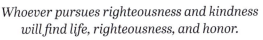

MONDAY, JUNE 10

Whoever pursues righteousness and kindness
will find life, righteousness, and honor.
PROVERBS 21:21 ESV

When I show kindness, often it is merely a reaction to my circumstances. I'm in the right place at the right time, so it's easy to help. But to be more like You, God, I will pursue kindness. I will seek out places to show Your goodness on a personal level. These things will bring glory to You, and that is what I want more than anything. . . .

PRAYER REQUESTS

ANSWERS TO PRAYER

PRAISES

TUESDAY, JUNE 11

*"Give to those who ask, and don't turn away
from those who want to borrow."*
MATTHEW 5:42 NLT

Asking for help is difficult, Lord, so I will not take it lightly when someone asks something of me. Whether it's money or things or my time, I will give joyfully and without reservation because You are so good to me. I will hold my possessions with an open hand rather than a tight grip because You own it all—I am just the caretaker. . . .

PRAYER REQUESTS

PRAISES

ANSWERS TO PRAYER

WEDNESDAY, JUNE 12

We should help others do what is right and build them up in the Lord.
ROMANS 15:2 NLT

Father, I am thankful You do not leave me where I am. I have Your Word to teach me Your ways, and You have given me mentors who encourage me to grow in my faith and maturity as Your daughter. Help me form relationships so I can build up others with that same encouragement to grow to be more like You every day. . . .

PRAYER REQUESTS

ANSWERS TO PRAYER

PRAISES

THURSDAY, JUNE 13

Help each other in troubles and problems.
This is the kind of law Christ asks us to obey.
GALATIANS 6:2 NLV

Lord God, make me a helper. When I see someone struggling, give me a nudge to act and act quickly—not in reckless haste, but in swift efficiency. Give me the wisdom to do the most helpful thing first. Inhabit my words so that Your Spirit can be at the center of my conversations. And when I need help, please send help quickly. . . .

PRAYER REQUESTS

PRAISES

ANSWERS TO PRAYER

FRIDAY, JUNE 14

Flag Day

"This is what the LORD of Heaven's Armies says:
Judge fairly, and show mercy and kindness to one another."

ZECHARIAH 7:9 NLT

Lord, I admit that sometimes I am not kind to the people I see every day. My attitude at home could use an adjustment. My mood around coworkers sometimes stinks. I say things I don't mean and have immediate regrets. When I react to my circumstances, help me to react as You do—with kindness, mercy, and fairness. . . .

PRAYER REQUESTS

ANSWERS TO PRAYER

PRAISES

SATURDAY, JUNE 15

Love each other with genuine affection,
and take delight in honoring each other.
ROMANS 12:10 NLT

God, when I see something good happen for someone else, I want to be a person who immediately joins the celebration with them! Take away any feelings of jealousy or thoughts of "Why not me?" and fill me with genuine happiness for them. When one person benefits, we can all take part in the joy. Thank You for Your blessings, because they are deep and wide. . . .

PRAYER REQUESTS

PRAISES

ANSWERS TO PRAYER

SUNDAY, JUNE 16

Father's Day

*See what kind of love the Father has given to us,
that we should be called children of God; and so we are.*

1 JOHN 3:1 ESV

God, today I celebrate my father. Thank You for his passions and talents and the influence he has on our family. He is strong. He is capable. He is a man who has taken care of me. He isn't perfect, but he is perfectly loved by You (and me). Please bless him today and every day. . . .

PRAYER REQUESTS

ANSWERS TO PRAYER

PRAISES

MONDAY, JUNE 17

Rejoice with those who rejoice, and weep with those who weep.
ROMANS 12:15 SKJV

Make me more in tune with the people around me, God. I don't want to be so wrapped up in my own selfishness that I miss the opportunity to experience the highs and lows with them. In times of celebration, make me the party planner. And in times of sorrow, let me be the shoulder to cry on. Thank You for doing the same for me. . . .

PRAYER REQUESTS

PRAISES

ANSWERS TO PRAYER

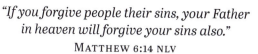

TUESDAY, JUNE 18

"If you forgive people their sins, your Father
in heaven will forgive your sins also."
MATTHEW 6:14 NLV

Soften my heart toward people who have wronged me, Father. When I think that holding a grudge will feel good, remind me that it does nothing but make me a slave to unforgiveness. I will forgive, knowing that it leads to freedom. I will forgive, knowing that You are faithful to forgive my many sins fully and absolutely. Thank You, Father. . . .

PRAYER REQUESTS

ANSWERS
TO PRAYER

PRAISES

WEDNESDAY, JUNE 19

"You have heard the law that says, 'Love your neighbor' and hate your enemy. But I say, love your enemies! Pray for those who persecute you!"
MATTHEW 5:43–44 NLT

It's easy for me to love some people, Lord. But You call me to a higher love, a deeper love. Change my heart toward the people I struggle with. Help me to see them as You see them. Help me to pray good for them and to do good to them, no matter how they treat me. . . .

PRAYER REQUESTS

PRAISES

ANSWERS TO PRAYER

THURSDAY, JUNE 20

First Day of Summer

Try to understand other people. Forgive each other.
If you have something against someone, forgive
him. That is the way the Lord forgave you.
COLOSSIANS 3:13 NLV

It's exhausting to keep score in relationships, God. So I'm laying it down at Your feet, and I will forgive so I can experience true freedom in my relationships and with You. Thank You, Father, for setting the example for me to learn *how* to forgive. You are the best teacher and friend. . . .

PRAYER REQUESTS

ANSWERS
TO PRAYER

PRAISES

FRIDAY, JUNE 21

A soft answer turns away wrath, but harsh words stir up anger.
PROVERBS 15:1 SKJV

Inhabit my words today, Lord. When I am stressed and an unkind response springs to my lips, help me to pause before hurling words that will discourage, tear down, frustrate, and anger. I need the Holy Spirit's help so I will speak in ways that encourage, uplift, refresh, and restore instead. I want the words that come out of my mouth to be Your words, God. . . .

PRAYER REQUESTS

PRAISES

ANSWERS TO PRAYER

SATURDAY, JUNE 22

So let's not get tired of doing what is good. At just the right time we will reap a harvest of blessing if we don't give up.

GALATIANS 6:9 NLT

I will not stop doing good for those around me, God. On days when it feels too difficult or inconvenient, remind me of the unending goodness that You shower on me. Give me the desire to multiply kindness and generosity and to encourage others to come alongside me to do the same. . . .

PRAYER REQUESTS

ANSWERS TO PRAYER

PRAISES

SUNDAY, JUNE 23

*Dear brothers and sisters, if another believer is overcome
by some sin, you who are godly should gently and
humbly help that person back onto the right path.*

GALATIANS 6:1 NLT

Confrontation is hard, Lord. So today, I ask for guidance from the Holy Spirit. If You want me to confront a friend who is struggling to stay on Your path, lead me in love and kindness. And if I am not the person You want to confront them, I will continue to pray for the situation. . . .

PRAYER REQUESTS

PRAISES

ANSWERS TO PRAYER

MONDAY, JUNE 24

*Pure and genuine religion in the sight of God
the Father means caring for orphans and widows in
their distress and refusing to let the world corrupt you.*
JAMES 1:27 NLT

You are a good Father to everyone, Lord, but You care especially for those who have lost fathers and husbands. I want to join You in that care of these souls. Give me opportunities to show kindness, support, and help whenever and wherever there are needs. . . .

PRAYER REQUESTS

ANSWERS TO PRAYER

PRAISES

TUESDAY, JUNE 25

*They should be rich in good works and generous to those
in need, always being ready to share with others.*

1 Timothy 6:18 NLT

I will not underestimate the power of sharing with others, God. You have given me so much, so I will share my abundance with those who have need. Make my heart willing and pliable in Your hands to give freely and without judging the person's situation or motive. Let my generosity spill over into every area of my life. . . .

PRAYER REQUESTS

PRAISES

ANSWERS TO PRAYER

"Give to anyone who asks; and when things are taken away from you, don't try to get them back."
Luke 6:30 NLT

When I was a toddler, nobody had to teach me the word *mine*. A toy? Mine! A favorite snack? Mine! As an adult, I sometimes suffer from the same selfishness, but I know in my heart that everything I have belongs to You, Father. Teach me how You want me to use Your money, possessions, and resources. . . .

PRAYER REQUESTS

ANSWERS TO PRAYER

PRAISES

THURSDAY, JUNE 27

"Your heart will be wherever your riches are."
LUKE 12:34 NLV

Lord, please give me an eternal perspective when it comes to money and posses-sions. Give me the wisdom to invest in Your people and Your kingdom and Your will rather than be tempted by the sparkle of temporary diversions and status symbols. Help me to see investment opportunities through Your eyes and to know the importance of quality over quantity and to appreciate the beauty of Your plan. . . .

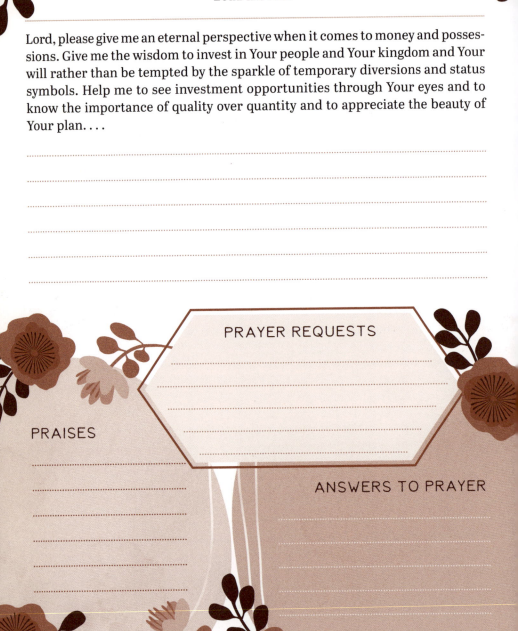

PRAYER REQUESTS

PRAISES

ANSWERS TO PRAYER

FRIDAY, JUNE 28

Never let loyalty and kindness leave you! Tie them around your neck as a reminder. Write them deep within your heart.
PROVERBS 3:3 NLT

I want to be a loyal friend, Father. Help me to keep my commitments to the relationships You have put in my life. I want to be present, compassionate, kind, and available. And please send loyal friends who will be rock solid for me. Thank You for being my loyal friend, committed to our relationship for all eternity. . . .

PRAYER REQUESTS

ANSWERS TO PRAYER

PRAISES

SATURDAY, JUNE 29

Don't just pretend to love others. Really love them. . . .
Love each other with genuine affection,
and take delight in honoring each other.
ROMANS 12:9–10 NLT

I will be a genuine friend, Lord. Please send me friends who are just as authentic. Relationships are not a show to impress others but deep heart connections that add so much to life. Strengthen my bond with the people You have put in my life, and give me opportunities to make new friends throughout my life. . . .

PRAYER REQUESTS

PRAISES

ANSWERS TO PRAYER

SUNDAY, JUNE 30

She opens her mouth with wisdom.
The teaching of kindness is on her tongue.
PROVERBS 31:26 NLV

Thank You, Father, for giving me examples in my life of truly kind women who embody the character of the Proverbs 31 woman. Help me to emulate the way they speak to others, constantly building up rather than tearing down. I hear Your wisdom when they talk, and I always come away feeling blessed. These women are a blessing to everyone they meet. . . .

PRAYER REQUESTS

ANSWERS
TO PRAYER

PRAISES

July

THE GIFT OF HOPE

And so, Lord, where do I put my hope?
My only hope is in you.
PSALM 39:7 NLT

SUNDAY	MONDAY	TUESDAY	WEDNESDAY	THURSDAY	FRIDAY	SATURDAY
	1	2	3	4 Independence Day	5	6
7	8	9	10	11	12	13
14	15	16	17	18	19	20
21	22	23	24	25	26	27
28	29	30	31			

The gift of hope is the gift of Jesus Christ. Because He took our sin upon Him on the cross and died and rose again, we can trust Him for salvation. No one but Jesus can promise us eternal life and a perfect future in heaven. Our only real hope is in Him, both now and forever!

MONDAY, JULY 1

Blessed be the God and Father of our Lord Jesus Christ! According to his great mercy, he has caused us to be born again to a living hope through the resurrection of Jesus Christ from the dead, to an inheritance that is imperishable, undefiled, and unfading, kept in heaven for you, who by God's power are being guarded through faith for a salvation ready to be revealed in the last time.

1 Peter 1:3–5 ESV

Heavenly Father, I'm so grateful for the living hope that I have in Jesus Christ. I thank You and praise You! . . .

PRAYER REQUESTS

ANSWERS TO PRAYER

PRAISES

TUESDAY, JULY 2

Now may the God of hope fill you with all joy and peace in believing,
that you may abound in hope through the power of the Holy Spirit.
ROMANS 15:13 SKJV

I'm grateful for You, God of hope! Sometimes I stop in awe and wonder, marveling over the fact that I am so blessed to have faith in You. So many people refuse to believe, and it's heartbreaking. Yet, I abound in hope through the power of Your Holy Spirit because of my salvation through Jesus Christ. Help me to do whatever I can to help lead others to faith, salvation, and hope too. . . .

PRAYER REQUESTS

PRAISES

ANSWERS TO PRAYER

WEDNESDAY, JULY 3

I will lift up my eyes to the mountains. Where will my help come from? My help comes from the Lord, Who made heaven and earth. He will not let your feet go out from under you. He Who watches over you will not sleep.... The Lord will watch over your coming and going, now and forever.

PSALM 121:1–3, 8 NLV

Lord, I look up to You for my help and hope. I lie down in peace at night, knowing You never stop watching over me. . . .

PRAYER REQUESTS

ANSWERS TO PRAYER

PRAISES

THURSDAY, JULY 4

Independence Day

For all creation is waiting eagerly for that future day when God will reveal who his children really are. Against its will, all creation was subjected to God's curse. But with eager hope, the creation looks forward to the day when it will join God's children in glorious freedom from death and decay.

ROMANS 8:19–21 NLT

I believe, God, that total and forever freedom from the death and decay and sadness of this world is coming! I have great hope and expectation because You always keep Your promises. . . .

PRAYER REQUESTS

PRAISES

ANSWERS TO PRAYER

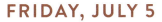

FRIDAY, JULY 5

I pray that your hearts will be flooded with light so that you can understand the confident hope he has given to those he called— his holy people who are his rich and glorious inheritance. I also pray that you will understand the incredible greatness of God's power for us who believe him. This is the same mighty power that raised Christ from the dead and seated him in the place of honor at God's right hand in the heavenly realms.

EPHESIANS 1:18–20 NLT

Lord, flood my heart with the light of understanding. Grow my confidence in the hope and power You give me. . . .

PRAYER REQUESTS

ANSWERS TO PRAYER

PRAISES

SATURDAY, JULY 6

*But you belong to God, my dear children. You have already
won a victory over those people, because the Spirit who lives
in you is greater than the spirit who lives in the world.*

1 John 4:4 NLT

Heavenly Father, thank You that I am Your child. I belong to You, and Your Holy
Spirit within me is always greater than the spirit of the world. With You, I can
overcome anything. . . .

PRAYER REQUESTS

PRAISES

ANSWERS TO PRAYER

SUNDAY, JULY 7

I will honor the Lord at all times. His praise will always be in my mouth. My soul will be proud to tell about the Lord. Let those who suffer hear it and be filled with joy. Give great honor to the Lord with me. Let us praise His name together.

PSALM 34:1–3 NLV

Lord, I want to tell others all about You! I want to be filled with great hope by choosing praise and prayer and keeping them in my mind and on my lips. . . .

PRAYER REQUESTS

ANSWERS TO PRAYER

PRAISES

MONDAY, JULY 8

If then you have been raised with Christ, seek the things that are above, where Christ is, seated at the right hand of God. Set your minds on things that are above, not on things that are on earth.

COLOSSIANS 3:1–2 ESV

Jesus, I seek the things above—where You are seated at the right hand of God. My hope is in You, not in the things here on earth. . . .

PRAYER REQUESTS

PRAISES

ANSWERS TO PRAYER

TUESDAY, JULY 9

Let us hold fast the confession of our hope without wavering, for he who promised is faithful. And let us consider how to stir up one another to love and good works, not neglecting to meet together, as is the habit of some, but encouraging one another, and all the more as you see the Day drawing near.

HEBREWS 10:23–25 ESV

I'm holding on tight to my faith and hope in You, Jesus, because You are faithful and true. Please let fellow believers encourage me, just as I encourage them— and all the more as we eagerly await Your return. . . .

PRAYER REQUESTS

ANSWERS TO PRAYER

PRAISES

WEDNESDAY, JULY 10

Behold, the eye of the Lord is on those who fear him, on those who hope in his steadfast love, that he may deliver their soul from death and keep them alive in famine. Our soul waits for the Lord; he is our help and our shield. For our heart is glad in him, because we trust in his holy name. Let your steadfast love, O Lord, be upon us, even as we hope in you.

PSALM 33:18–22 ESV

There is such comfort and strength in this psalm, Lord. I feel so protected and loved as I put my hope in You. . . .

PRAYER REQUESTS

PRAISES

ANSWERS TO PRAYER

THURSDAY, JULY 11

The people recognized Jesus at once, and they ran throughout the whole area, carrying sick people on mats to wherever they heard he was. Wherever he went—in villages, cities, or the countryside—they brought the sick out to the marketplaces. They begged him to let the sick touch at least the fringe of his robe, and all who touched him were healed.

MARK 6:54–56 NLT

I have hope for physical healing because of Your love and power, Jesus! Whether it is Your will for healing here on earth now or in heaven forever, I trust in You completely. . . .

PRAYER REQUESTS

ANSWERS TO PRAYER

PRAISES

FRIDAY, JULY 12

Those in need will not always be forgotten. The hope of the poor will not be lost forever. Rise up, O Lord! Do not let man win the fight against You. Let the nations come to You and be judged. Make them afraid, O Lord. Let the nations know they are only men.
PSALM 9:18–20 NLV

When it seems like evil in this world is winning, Lord, remind me that You will ultimately prevail. You are right and just and good. You will judge and punish and reward. You will make all things right one day soon. . . .

PRAYER REQUESTS

PRAISES

ANSWERS TO PRAYER

SATURDAY, JULY 13

Do all things without grumbling or disputing, that you may be blameless and innocent, children of God without blemish in the midst of a crooked and twisted generation, among whom you shine as lights in the world.

PHILIPPIANS 2:14–15 ESV

Heavenly Father, please help me to shine Your light of hope in the darkness of sin around me in this world. I want to shine brightly so others might come to know Jesus as Savior too. . . .

PRAYER REQUESTS

ANSWERS TO PRAYER

PRAISES

SUNDAY, JULY 14

"God is not man, that he should lie, or a son of man, that he should change his mind. Has he said, and will he not do it? Or has he spoken, and will he not fulfill it?"
NUMBERS 23:19 ESV

Father, since people have let me down, sometimes I wonder if You will let me down. So please remind me that You are not a mere man. You don't ever lie or break Your promises. My hope and trust are always secure in You. . . .

PRAYER REQUESTS

PRAISES

ANSWERS TO PRAYER

MONDAY, JULY 15

By day the LORD went ahead of them in a pillar of cloud to guide them on their way and by night in a pillar of fire to give them light, so that they could travel by day or night. Neither the pillar of cloud by day nor the pillar of fire by night left its place in front of the people.

EXODUS 13:21–22 NIV

Lord, when I'm not exactly sure the way to go, I will not lose hope. I trust You will lead me in miraculous ways. . . .

PRAYER REQUESTS

ANSWERS TO PRAYER

PRAISES

TUESDAY, JULY 16

"I will show you what it's like when someone comes to me, listens to my teaching, and then follows it. It is like a person building a house who digs deep and lays the foundation on solid rock. When the floodwaters rise and break against that house, it stands firm because it is well built."

LUKE 6:47–48 NLT

I have hope and stability through all the storms of life because You are my foundation, Jesus. I follow You, and I will stand firm upon my faith in You. . . .

PRAYER REQUESTS

PRAISES

ANSWERS TO PRAYER

WEDNESDAY, JULY 17

If you, Lord, should write down our sins, O Lord, who could stand?
But You are the One Who forgives, so You are honored with fear.
I wait for the Lord. My soul waits and I hope in His Word.
PSALM 130:3–5 NLV

I would be lost and hopeless, stuck in my sins without You, Lord. But when I ask You for forgiveness, You erase my sins. You do not hold them against me. I'm so grateful for the privilege of loving You and hoping in You! . . .

PRAYER REQUESTS

ANSWERS TO PRAYER

PRAISES

THURSDAY, JULY 18

I will call to you whenever I'm in trouble, and you will answer me. No pagan god is like you, O Lord. None can do what you do! All the nations you made will come and bow before you, Lord; they will praise your holy name. For you are great and perform wonderful deeds. You alone are God.

PSALM 86:7–10 NLT

Lord, I believe wholeheartedly that You alone are the one true God. There is no real, eternal hope in anyone or anything but You! I trust in You alone. . . .

PRAYER REQUESTS

PRAISES

ANSWERS TO PRAYER

FRIDAY, JULY 19

Then the word of the LORD came to [Elijah]: "Go at once to Zarephath in the region of Sidon and stay there. I have directed a widow there to supply you with food."

1 KINGS 17:8–9 NIV

Heavenly Father, when I feel desperate and hopeless, remind me how You provided for Elijah. I pray that You will provide for me in miraculous ways. I believe You can and will. . . .

PRAYER REQUESTS

ANSWERS TO PRAYER

PRAISES

SATURDAY, JULY 20

"Physical training is good, but training for godliness is much better, promising benefits in this life and in the life to come." This is a trustworthy saying, and everyone should accept it. This is why we work hard and continue to struggle, for our hope is in the living God.

1 TIMOTHY 4:8–10 NLT

Heavenly Father, remind me that putting my hope in health and physical fitness in this world will ultimately disappoint. While taking care of myself is of course important, even more important is being trained in godliness. Please make me more and more like Jesus. . . .

PRAYER REQUESTS

PRAISES

ANSWERS TO PRAYER

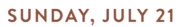

SUNDAY, JULY 21

*"But forget all that—it is nothing compared to what I am going
to do. For I am about to do something new. See, I have already
begun! Do you not see it? I will make a pathway through the
wilderness. I will create rivers in the dry wasteland."*

ISAIAH 43:18–19 NLT

Heavenly Father, please help me to let go of the past and focus with great hope
and confidence on the awesome new things You are doing. Please fill my life with
Your good blessings. . . .

PRAYER REQUESTS

ANSWERS
TO PRAYER

PRAISES

MONDAY, JULY 22

For he will command his angels concerning you to guard
you in all your ways. On their hands they will bear
you up, lest you strike your foot against a stone.
PSALM 91:11–12 ESV

Heavenly Father, thank You for Your mighty angels who obey Your commands and who watch over me. I feel secure and loved, full of hope and peace because of Your care and protection. . . .

PRAYER REQUESTS

PRAISES

ANSWERS TO PRAYER

TUESDAY, JULY 23

There is one hope in which you were called. There is one Lord and one faith and one baptism. There is one God. He is the Father of us all. He is over us all. He is the One working through us all. He is the One living in us all.

Ephesians 4:4–6 nlv

Remind me that this hope I have in You is both incredible and simple, Lord. You are the *one* true God, and my one main focus in life should be worshipping and loving and living for You. . . .

PRAYER REQUESTS

ANSWERS TO PRAYER

PRAISES

WEDNESDAY, JULY 24

Now we are children of God, and what we will be has not yet been made known. But we know that when Christ appears, we shall be like him, for we shall see him as he is. All who have this hope in him purify themselves, just as he is pure.

1 JOHN 3:2–3 NIV

Heavenly Father, I have great hope for what is yet to come because I am Your child. When Christ appears, I will be like Him, and I stand in awe and wonder and excitement of that precious promise! . . .

PRAYER REQUESTS

PRAISES

ANSWERS TO PRAYER

THURSDAY, JULY 25

*Show me your ways, LORD, teach me your paths. Guide
me in your truth and teach me, for you are God my Savior,
and my hope is in you all day long. Remember, LORD,
your great mercy and love, for they are from of old.*
PSALM 25:4–6 NIV

As I keep my faith and hope in You, Lord, please guide me. Teach me what I need
to know. Help me to follow You on the right paths. Show me Your ways, and help
me point others to You. . . .

PRAYER REQUESTS

ANSWERS
TO PRAYER

PRAISES

FRIDAY, JULY 26

Even when there was no reason for hope, Abraham kept hoping—
believing that he would become the father of many nations. For God
had said to him, "That's how many descendants you will have!"
And Abraham's faith did not weaken, even though, at about 100
years of age, he figured his body was as good as dead—and so was
Sarah's womb. Abraham never wavered in believing God's promise.
In fact, his faith grew stronger, and in this he brought glory to God.
ROMANS 4:18–20 NLT

Lord, help me to be more like Abraham, with unwavering faith and hope
in You. . . .

PRAYER REQUESTS

PRAISES

ANSWERS TO PRAYER

SATURDAY, JULY 27

A woman who had suffered from a discharge of blood for twelve years came up behind him and touched the fringe of his garment, for she said to herself, "If I only touch his garment, I will be made well." Jesus turned, and seeing her he said, "Take heart, daughter; your faith has made you well." And instantly the woman was made well.

MATTHEW 9:20–22 ESV

Jesus, I take heart and have hope in You alone. You have all power to heal and to give eternal life. I praise You for this awesome truth! . . .

PRAYER REQUESTS

ANSWERS TO PRAYER

PRAISES

SUNDAY, JULY 28

All at once [Saul] saw a light from heaven shining around him. He fell to the ground. Then he heard a voice say, "Saul, Saul, why are you working so hard against Me?" Saul answered, "Who are You, Lord?" He said, "I am Jesus, the One Whom you are working against. You hurt yourself by trying to hurt Me." Saul was shaken and surprised. Then he said, "What do You want me to do, Lord?"

ACTS 9:3–6 NLV

Lord, the total transformation of Saul reminds me that there is hope for any and every person to be changed and to turn and follow You. . . .

PRAYER REQUESTS

PRAISES

ANSWERS TO PRAYER

MONDAY, JULY 29

Why are you sad, O my soul? Why have you become
troubled within me? Hope in God, for I will praise
Him again for His help of being near me.
PSALM 42:5 NLV

Lord, when I am sad and troubled in my soul, please help me put my hope back in You. Help me to remember Your goodness and power and all You have done for me in the past, so that I will refocus on trusting You for the present and the future. . . .

PRAYER REQUESTS

ANSWERS
TO PRAYER

PRAISES

TUESDAY, JULY 30

I remember my affliction and my wandering, the bitterness and the gall. I well remember them, and my soul is downcast within me. Yet this I call to mind and therefore I have hope: because of the LORD's great love we are not consumed, for his compassions never fail. They are new every morning; great is your faithfulness.

LAMENTATIONS 3:19–23 NIV

I too remember well the hard times in my life, Lord. Yet, I also remember Your great love and care that helped me through them. And so I continue to hope in You. Great is Your faithfulness! . . .

PRAYER REQUESTS

PRAISES

ANSWERS TO PRAYER

WEDNESDAY, JULY 31

Put all your hope in the gracious salvation that will come to you when Jesus Christ is revealed to the world. So you must live as God's obedient children. Don't slip back into your old ways of living to satisfy your own desires. You didn't know any better then. But now you must be holy in everything you do, just as God who chose you is holy.

1 PETER 1:13–15 NLT

Because all my hope is in the gracious salvation You have given me, Jesus, I want to live with obedience, self-control, and holiness to honor You and show my love and gratitude for You. . . .

PRAYER REQUESTS

ANSWERS TO PRAYER

PRAISES

August

A FOUNDATION OF FAITHFULNESS

Trust in the LORD with all your heart and do not lean on your own understanding. In all your ways acknowledge Him, and He shall direct your paths.

PROVERBS 3:5–6 SKJV

SUNDAY	MONDAY	TUESDAY	WEDNESDAY	THURSDAY	FRIDAY	SATURDAY
				1	2	3
4	5	6	7	8	9	10
11	12	13	14	15	16	17
18	19	20	21	22	23	24
25	26	27	28	29	30	31

God is intimately involved in your everyday life. When you see and acknowledge Him working, it can motivate you to pray for His direction, strengthening your faith in Him. Today, let your roots grow deeper as you learn to trust Him more and more.

THURSDAY, AUGUST 1

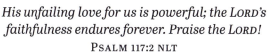

His unfailing love for us is powerful; the LORD's
faithfulness endures forever. Praise the LORD!
PSALM 117:2 NLT

I praise You, almighty God, for Your commitment to loving me unconditionally. Sometimes I don't even like myself, but Your all-encompassing, powerful love for me never falters. You never waver or withhold Your care for me. There is no lapse in the timeline of Your faithfulness to me. I cannot fully understand it, but I am grateful for it. . . .

PRAYER REQUESTS

ANSWERS
TO PRAYER

PRAISES

FRIDAY, AUGUST 2

"And whatever you ask in prayer,
you will receive, if you have faith."
MATTHEW 21:22 ESV

Father, I ask for a lot in prayer. Sometimes I think I am asking too much, but then scripture reminds me that whatever I ask, I will receive if I have faith. I have faith that You hear me, Lord. I have faith that Your timing is perfect. I have faith that Your will is best and that You will do it. Align my request with Your plan, Lord. . . .

PRAYER REQUESTS

PRAISES

ANSWERS TO PRAYER

SATURDAY, AUGUST 3

And it is impossible to please God without faith. Anyone
who wants to come to him must believe that God exists
and that he rewards those who sincerely seek him.
HEBREWS 11:6 NLT

I earnestly want to please You, God. I believe in You. I know You are good. I trust that Your plan is the best thing for me. And I want more of You. Please help my faith grow stronger, rooted more deeply in You. May Your Spirit come alive inside my heart today. . . .

PRAYER REQUESTS

ANSWERS TO PRAYER

PRAISES

SUNDAY, AUGUST 4

"Have faith in God. I tell you the truth, you can say to this mountain, 'May you be lifted up and thrown into the sea,' and it will happen. But you must really believe it will happen and have no doubt in your heart."

MARK 11:22–23 NLT

Lord God, I don't understand how powerful, mountain-moving faith works, but Your promise is amazing to me! I believe You can do anything. And I also believe You can do anything through me. Remove all doubt from my heart. . . .

PRAYER REQUESTS

PRAISES

ANSWERS TO PRAYER

MONDAY, AUGUST 5

God saved you by his grace when you believed. And you can't take credit for this; it is a gift from God. Salvation is not a reward for the good things we have done, so none of us can boast about it.
EPHESIANS 2:8–9 NLT

I am humbled by Your grace, God. When I start to feel proud of the good things I do, remind me that it is only because of Your gracious gift of salvation that I am saved from eternity apart from You. . . .

PRAYER REQUESTS

ANSWERS TO PRAYER

PRAISES

TUESDAY, AUGUST 6

Our life is lived by faith. We do not live by what we see in front of us.
2 CORINTHIANS 5:7 NLV

Lord, strengthen my faith when I feel doubt start to creep in—when my mind tells me that I need to see physical evidence to trust that You've got everything handled. That's just my sinful nature trying to take control. Instead, I will choose to live a life of faith, believing in Your everlasting presence and love for me....

PRAYER REQUESTS

PRAISES

ANSWERS TO PRAYER

WEDNESDAY, AUGUST 7

Now someone may argue, "Some people have faith; others have good deeds." But I say, "How can you show me your faith if you don't have good deeds? I will show you my faith by my good deeds."

JAMES 2:18 NLT

I want my faith to go hand in hand with good works, Father. I am saved through faith, but I also know that doing good deeds in Your name is the best way to share Your love with others. Give me opportunities to do just that. . . .

PRAYER REQUESTS

ANSWERS TO PRAYER

PRAISES

THURSDAY, AUGUST 8

"I tell you the truth, if you had faith even as small as a mustard seed, you could say to this mountain, 'Move from here to there,' and it would move. Nothing would be impossible."

MATTHEW 17:20 NLT

Nothing is impossible. When I am feeling frustrated and stagnant and think that nothing will ever change, remind me of those words. Strengthen my faith so I can speak change and believe wholeheartedly that You will make it so. . . .

PRAYER REQUESTS

PRAISES

ANSWERS TO PRAYER

FRIDAY, AUGUST 9

I have fought a good fight. I have finished
the work I was to do. I have kept the faith.
2 Timothy 4:7 NLV

No matter what is happening around me, Lord, I will keep my faith. It is my anchor in the storm. It is the buoy of hope in the deepest waters. It helps me stay focused on both eternity and the here and now. Faith in You is my greatest treasure. . . .

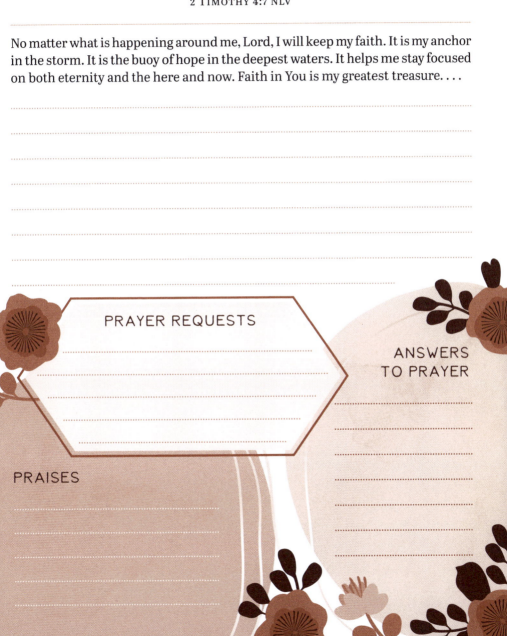

PRAYER REQUESTS

ANSWERS
TO PRAYER

PRAISES

SATURDAY, AUGUST 10

Be on your guard; stand firm in the faith; be courageous; be strong.
1 Corinthians 16:13 niv

Father, You have equipped me to be strong in You. I have Your Word to encourage me when I am struggling. I have friends who love You and love me and help me when I need an extra boost. Your promises help me through hard times. You have made me strong so I can courageously lead others who need extra encouragement today. . . .

PRAYER REQUESTS

PRAISES

ANSWERS TO PRAYER

SUNDAY, AUGUST 11

And Jesus said to him, "Go, for your faith has healed you."
Instantly the man could see, and he followed Jesus down the road.
MARK 10:52 NLT

I want the healing kind of faith that this blind man had, Jesus. Give me the sort of belief in You that is deep enough and wide enough to change the course of my life for good. When I am living in Your will, I know I will see amazing, miraculous things happen. . . .

PRAYER REQUESTS

ANSWERS
TO PRAYER

PRAISES

MONDAY, AUGUST 12

*If you declare with your mouth, "Jesus is Lord," and believe in
your heart that God raised him from the dead, you will be saved.*

ROMANS 10:9 NIV

Jesus, You are King over all, and I commit my life to You. Please be the Lord of my
heart, my thoughts, my actions, and my beliefs. You are worthy to oversee it all.
Your sacrifice on the cross and comeback from the grave gives You the authority.
Thank You for taking care of everything. . . .

PRAYER REQUESTS

PRAISES

ANSWERS TO PRAYER

TUESDAY, AUGUST 13

In all circumstances take up the shield of faith, with which you can extinguish all the flaming darts of the evil one.
Ephesians 6:16 esv

When I feel like my beliefs are under attack, God, help me to use Your protection of the shield of faith. My relationship with You is more than just a surface-level friendship. It's a life-giving connection, an essential part of who I am. I will stand firm and shield myself and the people I love from the attacks of evil. . . .

PRAYER REQUESTS

ANSWERS
TO PRAYER

PRAISES

WEDNESDAY, AUGUST 14

For you know that when your faith is tested,
your endurance has a chance to grow.
JAMES 1:3 NLT

I would never ask for trials, Father, but I know they will come. And when they do, help me keep the proper perspective, knowing they will not last forever and that You will help me endure the hard times. Even better, You will increase my endurance and give me compassion toward others whose faith is being tested as well. . . .

PRAYER REQUESTS

PRAISES

ANSWERS TO PRAYER

THURSDAY, AUGUST 15

Let us keep looking to Jesus. Our faith comes from Him and He is the One Who makes it perfect. He did not give up when He had to suffer shame and die on a cross. He knew of the joy that would be His later. Now He is sitting at the right side of God.

HEBREWS 12:2 NLV

My faith isn't perfected because of anything I have done, Jesus. I know it is because You were willing to do the Father's will. . . .

PRAYER REQUESTS

ANSWERS TO PRAYER

PRAISES

FRIDAY, AUGUST 16

Fight the good fight of faith. Take hold of the life that lasts forever. You were chosen to receive it. You have spoken well about this life in front of many people.

1 TIMOTHY 6:12 NLV

When times are tough, I will fight to keep my faith. I will fight for the faith of the people I love. You want to see me succeed, Father, and I know You are my biggest proponent and cheerleader. Help me to see the big picture instead of getting discouraged in the fight today. . . .

PRAYER REQUESTS

PRAISES

ANSWERS TO PRAYER

SATURDAY, AUGUST 17

"I am the resurrection and the life. The one who believes in me will live, even though they die; and whoever lives by believing in me will never die. Do you believe this?"

JOHN 11:25–26 NIV

Lord, Your promise of eternal life is one of the biggest reasons for my hope. This broken, hurting world is not the beginning and the end. You came before this world, and You are planning the perfect place after this world in heaven. Help me to share that hope with others today. . . .

PRAYER REQUESTS

ANSWERS TO PRAYER

PRAISES

SUNDAY, AUGUST 18

Because Sarah had faith, she was able to have a child long after she was past the age to have children. She had faith to believe that God would do what He promised.

HEBREWS 11:11 NLV

Almighty God, please give me a faith like Sarah's. Give me wisdom to understand Your will; and when my circumstances seem impossible, when all the cards are stacked against me, help me to believe that You will do what You have promised. . . .

PRAYER REQUESTS

PRAISES

ANSWERS TO PRAYER

MONDAY, AUGUST 19

*You have never seen Him but you love Him. You cannot
see Him now but you are putting your trust in Him.
And you have joy so great that words cannot tell about it.*

1 Peter 1:8 NLV

Your love amazes me, Father. Your provision for my life—from the big things to the small details—makes me feel so cared for. You choose to call me Your child when I am at my best and when I'm at my worst. I am humbled and grateful. . . .

PRAYER REQUESTS

ANSWERS TO PRAYER

PRAISES

TUESDAY, AUGUST 20

*These trials will show that your faith is genuine. It is
being tested as fire tests and purifies gold—though
your faith is far more precious than mere gold.*

1 Peter 1:7 nlt

I want my faith to be the real thing, Lord. When difficult times come that test my
faith in You, please walk through the fire with me. Purify my faith in that process,
and let the impurities burn away, leaving me with a purer, stronger faith that will
withstand any difficulty. . . .

PRAYER REQUESTS

PRAISES

ANSWERS TO PRAYER

WEDNESDAY, AUGUST 21

*Pursue righteousness and a godly life, along with
faith, love, perseverance, and gentleness.*
1 TIMOTHY 6:11 NLT

The world tells me to pursue my own desires: money, fame, beauty—but all these things are temporary. The things You want me to pursue are eternal, Lord: righteousness, godly living, faith, love, perseverance, and gentleness. Give me the wisdom to know the difference between immediate gratification and long-term contentment and joy. With Your help, I will find these things in You, Father. . . .

PRAYER REQUESTS

ANSWERS
TO PRAYER

PRAISES

THURSDAY, AUGUST 22

For it is by believing in your heart that you are made right with God, and it is by openly declaring your faith that you are saved.

ROMANS 10:10 NLT

Being "right with God" sounds like a difficult task, Jesus. But the truth is that I can be right with You not by any effort on my part. I am in good standing with You because I believe in my heart that You died for my sins and because I have faith in Your promise of eternal life. . . .

PRAYER REQUESTS

PRAISES

ANSWERS TO PRAYER

FRIDAY, AUGUST 23

If someone asks about your hope as a believer,
always be ready to explain it.
1 PETER 3:15 NLT

I am not afraid to be asked about my faith, Lord. Because the truth is that my faith is who I am. I will always be ready to share how You have changed me for the good and how You are working in my life now. When I share my hope in You, please make the listener's ears open to hear Your truth. . . .

PRAYER REQUESTS

ANSWERS
TO PRAYER

PRAISES

SATURDAY, AUGUST 24

Therefore, since we have been made right in God's sight by faith, we have peace with God because of what Jesus Christ our Lord has done for us.

ROMANS 5:1 NLT

I am grateful for the security I have in my relationship with You, God. Your presence is a balm of peace in my heart, and I know I can talk to You about anything that is troubling me. You know me from the inside out. Help me grow to know You better. . . .

PRAYER REQUESTS

PRAISES

ANSWERS TO PRAYER

SUNDAY, AUGUST 25

*But Jesus turned around, and when He saw her, He said,
"Daughter, be of good comfort; your faith has healed
you." And the woman was healed from that hour.*
MATTHEW 9:22 SKJV

You are the Great Physician, Lord, and I need Your healing. Physically, emotionally, mentally, and spiritually, I need Your hand to guide my health to wholeness in You. I believe You can heal in an instant, and I believe You can heal over time. Please do a healing work in me. . . .

PRAYER REQUESTS

ANSWERS TO PRAYER

PRAISES

MONDAY, AUGUST 26

*"If you have faith as small as a mustard seed,
you can say to this mulberry tree, 'Be uprooted
and planted in the sea,' and it will obey you."*

Luke 17:6 niv

I believe my faith is at least as large as a tiny mustard seed, Lord. I say I believe with my mouth, and I own that belief in my heart. I believe Your power is greater than any impossibility. Help that faith to grow, rooted into Your Word and Your will for my life. . . .

PRAYER REQUESTS

PRAISES

ANSWERS TO PRAYER

TUESDAY, AUGUST 27

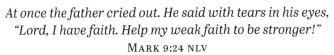

At once the father cried out. He said with tears in his eyes,
"Lord, I have faith. Help my weak faith to be stronger!"
MARK 9:24 NLV

When I feel my strength begin to falter, Jesus, build me up in faith. Let Your Spirit rattle my heart so I *feel* Your presence. I will not live a shrinking or stagnant faith. With Your help, my faith will grow stronger with each challenge and victory. I give You all the praise and glory. . . .

PRAYER REQUESTS

ANSWERS TO PRAYER

PRAISES

WEDNESDAY, AUGUST 28

Show other Christians how to live by your life. They should be able to follow you in the way you talk and in what you do. Show them how to live in faith and in love and in holy living.

1 TIMOTHY 4:12 NLV

Help me be an example of faith to others, God. I am not perfect, but I am made perfect in You. Give me words to encourage others and compassion for those who are struggling. You love them as much as You love me. . . .

PRAYER REQUESTS

PRAISES

ANSWERS TO PRAYER

THURSDAY, AUGUST 29

"I tell you the truth, anyone who believes has eternal life."
JOHN 6:47 NLT

Jesus, I love all Your promises, but my favorite is Your promise of eternal life. What's even more amazing and beautiful is that You tell me that when I believe, eternity starts *now*. Eternal life isn't something that begins after I die or at Your second coming. I'm experiencing Your eternal goodness in this moment and will keep experiencing it forever. Thank You, thank You, thank You! . . .

PRAYER REQUESTS

ANSWERS TO PRAYER

PRAISES

FRIDAY, AUGUST 30

And who can win this battle against the world?
Only those who believe that Jesus is the Son of God.
1 JOHN 5:5 NLT

Some days feel like I'm in the middle of a war zone, Lord. This world is full of sin, selfishness, heartache, tragedy, sickness, and death. While it seems like evil is winning today's battle, You are victorious in the war. I believe in You, Jesus, and I choose the side of right in this war. Thank You for already making me victorious! . . .

PRAYER REQUESTS

PRAISES

ANSWERS TO PRAYER

SATURDAY, AUGUST 31

For you are all children of God through faith in Christ Jesus.
GALATIANS 3:26 NLT

I am so blessed to be Your beloved daughter, God. The good gifts You give Your family are too many to count, but I will spend my days in praise of Your generosity. Thank You for giving me a place to belong. Thank You for the gift of grace. Thank You for giving me a hopeful future with You and a purpose to live today. You are so good to me. . . .

PRAYER REQUESTS

ANSWERS TO PRAYER

PRAISES

September

CELEBRATING DAILY BLESSINGS

Every good and perfect gift is from above, coming down
from the Father of the heavenly lights, who does
not change like shifting shadows.

JAMES 1:17 NIV

SUNDAY	MONDAY	TUESDAY	WEDNESDAY	THURSDAY	FRIDAY	SATURDAY
1	2 Labor Day	3	4	5	6	7
8	9	10	11	12	13	14
15	16	17	18	19	20	21
22 First Day of Autumn	23	24	25	26	27	28
29	30					

Simply taking a big deep breath is a blessing from God. Scripture tells us that "he himself gives everyone life and breath and everything else" (Acts 17:25 NIV). When we choose to focus on daily blessings, both big and small, we have every reason to celebrate with gratitude and to praise our good heavenly Father.

SUNDAY, SEPTEMBER 1

Thus says the LORD, your Redeemer, who formed you from the womb: "I am the LORD, who made all things, who alone stretched out the heavens, who spread out the earth by myself."
ISAIAH 44:24 ESV

Creator God, I thank and praise You for the awesome blessing of Your beautiful creation! You've made all things from the tiniest baby in the womb to the stars stretched out in the vast heavens. I am amazed by You. . . .

PRAYER REQUESTS

ANSWERS TO PRAYER

PRAISES

MONDAY, SEPTEMBER 2

Labor Day

*Work willingly at whatever you do, as though you were
working for the Lord rather than for people. Remember
that the Lord will give you an inheritance as your reward,
and that the Master you are serving is Christ.*

Colossians 3:23–24 NLT

Lord, thank You for the blessing of the ability to work. At any task or job, I want
to do my best as one who works for You as my loving Master. I want my efforts to
glorify Your great name. . . .

PRAYER REQUESTS

PRAISES

ANSWERS TO PRAYER

TUESDAY, SEPTEMBER 3

If any does not provide for his own, and especially for those of his own house, he has denied the faith and is worse than an unbeliever.

1 TIMOTHY 5:8 SKJV

Thank You for the precious people You have given me as family, Lord! Even through our ups and downs, they are such a dear blessing, and I don't want to take them for granted. Help us to love and care for each other well. . . .

PRAYER REQUESTS

ANSWERS TO PRAYER

PRAISES

WEDNESDAY, SEPTEMBER 4

A friend loves at all times. A brother is born to share troubles.
PROVERBS 17:17 NLV

Lord, You are so good to give me the gift of friendship. Thank You for creating people to need good relationships. It's so good to encourage others and be encouraged and simply to enjoy life with people who understand and appreciate and love me. Please bless my dear friends who are such a blessing to me. . . .

PRAYER REQUESTS

PRAISES

ANSWERS TO PRAYER

THURSDAY, SEPTEMBER 5

*God will supply every need of yours according
to his riches in glory in Christ Jesus.*
PHILIPPIANS 4:19 ESV

You've shown me the truth of this scripture time and time again, Father. Even when life is not going as I'd hoped and planned, I've never been without what I really need. I trust You and thank You for every blessing, both big and small. . . .

PRAYER REQUESTS

ANSWERS
TO PRAYER

PRAISES

FRIDAY, SEPTEMBER 6

*Jesus called a little child to him and put the child among them.
Then he said, "I tell you the truth, unless you turn from your
sins and become like little children, you will never get into the
Kingdom of Heaven. So anyone who becomes as humble as
this little child is the greatest in the Kingdom of Heaven."*

MATTHEW 18:2–4 NLT

Thank You for the sweet children in my life, Lord! Their love and honesty and
humility and enthusiasm are inspiring. Help me to be more like them in the ways
You want me to be childlike. . . .

PRAYER REQUESTS

PRAISES

ANSWERS TO PRAYER

SATURDAY, SEPTEMBER 7

For God is the one who provides seed for the farmer and then bread to eat. In the same way, he will provide and increase your resources and then produce a great harvest of generosity in you. Yes, you will be enriched in every way so that you can always be generous. And when we take your gifts to those who need them, they will thank God.

2 CORINTHIANS 9:10–11 NLT

God, thank You for my many blessings. You are generous and kind, and I want to be more and more like You. Help me to point others to You as I share my blessings. . . .

PRAYER REQUESTS

ANSWERS TO PRAYER

PRAISES

SUNDAY, SEPTEMBER 8

"Every moving thing that lives shall be food for you.
And as I gave you the green plants, I give you everything."
GENESIS 9:3 ESV

Creator God, thank You for the gift of all kinds of tasty food and the creativity of cooking it in delicious ways. Help me to always have enough yet not too much. Help me to share with others in need. And help me to be wise and healthy as I eat and drink and enjoy it. . . .

PRAYER REQUESTS

PRAISES

ANSWERS TO PRAYER

MONDAY, SEPTEMBER 9

*God has given each of you a gift from his great variety
of spiritual gifts. Use them well to serve one another. Do you
have the gift of speaking? Then speak as though God himself
were speaking through you. Do you have the gift of helping
others? Do it with all the strength and energy that God supplies.
Then everything you do will bring glory to God through Jesus Christ.*

1 PETER 4:10–11 NLT

Lord, thank You for blessing me with unique spiritual gifts. Help me to have confidence in them and to use them to serve others as You have planned. . . .

PRAYER REQUESTS

ANSWERS TO PRAYER

PRAISES

TUESDAY, SEPTEMBER 10

"Come to me, all who labor and are heavy laden, and I will give you rest. Take my yoke upon you, and learn from me, for I am gentle and lowly in heart, and you will find rest for your souls. For my yoke is easy, and my burden is light."

MATTHEW 11:28–30 ESV

Jesus, thank You for the blessing of rest. You don't expect me to be constantly working myself to weariness. You call me to relax in peaceful relationship with You as I continue to know and love You more and more. . . .

PRAYER REQUESTS

PRAISES

ANSWERS TO PRAYER

WEDNESDAY, SEPTEMBER 11

Dear friend, I pray that you may enjoy good health and that all may go well with you, even as your soul is getting along well.

3 JOHN 2 NIV

Heavenly Father, thank You for the blessing of good health. When I'm not in good health, thank You for the blessing of modern medicine and good medical care. And at all times, help me to remember that my life is in Your hands and You have promised me forever in heaven. . . .

PRAYER REQUESTS

ANSWERS TO PRAYER

PRAISES

THURSDAY, SEPTEMBER 12

Praise be to the God and Father of our Lord Jesus Christ,
the Father of compassion and the God of all comfort,
who comforts us in all our troubles, so that we can comfort those
in any trouble with the comfort we ourselves receive from God.
2 CORINTHIANS 1:3–4 NIV

Especially when life is sad and hard, Lord, thank You for the comfort You give and the comfort You provide through others who can empathize with my circumstances....

PRAYER REQUESTS

PRAISES

ANSWERS TO PRAYER

FRIDAY, SEPTEMBER 13

*From his abundance we have all received one gracious blessing
after another. For the law was given through Moses, but God's
unfailing love and faithfulness came through Jesus Christ.*
JOHN 1:16–17 NLT

I should stop to count my blessings more often than I do, Lord. You truly have
given me one gracious blessing after another in my life. Right now, I want to list
my many blessings and praise You for them with gratitude. . . .

PRAYER REQUESTS

ANSWERS
TO PRAYER

PRAISES

SATURDAY, SEPTEMBER 14

"Anyone who listens to my teaching and follows it is wise, like a person who builds a house on solid rock. Though the rain comes in torrents and the floodwaters rise and the winds beat against that house, it won't collapse because it is built on bedrock."

MATTHEW 7:24–25 NLT

Jesus, thank You that my life can be strong and steady because I'm building it on the rock-solid truth of Your Word. . . .

PRAYER REQUESTS

PRAISES

ANSWERS TO PRAYER

SUNDAY, SEPTEMBER 15

"Be faithful in obeying the Lord your God. Be careful to keep all His Laws which I tell you today. And the Lord your God will set you high above all the nations of the earth. All these good things will come upon you if you will obey the Lord your God."

DEUTERONOMY 28:1–2 NLV

Lord God, You are holy and worthy of all honor and praise and obedience. Please help me to remember that being obedient to You is the very best way to live—the way to true blessings, both now in this world and (more importantly) for eternity. . . .

PRAYER REQUESTS

ANSWERS TO PRAYER

PRAISES

MONDAY, SEPTEMBER 16

*So Jotham became mighty, because he
ordered his ways before the LORD his God.*
2 CHRONICLES 27:6 ESV

Lord God, like Jotham, I want to order my ways with You in mind. I want my life and my plans to bring glory to You. I believe there is no better blessing in life than to follow and obey You. . . .

PRAYER REQUESTS

PRAISES

ANSWERS TO PRAYER

TUESDAY, SEPTEMBER 17

"He will yet make you laugh and call out with joy."
JOB 8:21 NLV

Lord, thank You for the gift of laughter. So many stressful and hard situations are made better by simply finding the humor in them. And laughter makes life so much easier to enjoy. Thank You for blessing me with people in my life to laugh and joke and have fun with—in good ways that honor You. . . .

PRAYER REQUESTS

ANSWERS
TO PRAYER

PRAISES

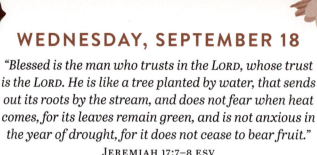

WEDNESDAY, SEPTEMBER 18

"Blessed is the man who trusts in the LORD, whose trust is the LORD. He is like a tree planted by water, that sends out its roots by the stream, and does not fear when heat comes, for its leaves remain green, and is not anxious in the year of drought, for it does not cease to bear fruit."
JEREMIAH 17:7–8 ESV

Lord, it's such a blessing simply to trust in You and to be strong and calm and steady because of my faith in and dependence on You. . . .

PRAYER REQUESTS

PRAISES

ANSWERS TO PRAYER

THURSDAY, SEPTEMBER 19

"'Lord, when did we ever see you hungry and feed you? Or thirsty and give you something to drink? Or a stranger and show you hospitality? Or naked and give you clothing? . . .' And the King will say, 'I tell you the truth, when you did it to one of the least of these my brothers and sisters, you were doing it to me!'"

MATTHEW 25:37–38, 40 NLT

Lord, thank You for the blessing and privilege of serving You by serving others and caring for their needs. . . .

PRAYER REQUESTS

ANSWERS TO PRAYER

PRAISES

FRIDAY, SEPTEMBER 20

"Give, and you will receive. Your gift will return to you in full—pressed down, shaken together to make room for more, running over, and poured into your lap. The amount you give will determine the amount you get back."
LUKE 6:38 NLT

Heavenly Father, remind me that as I give to others, I'm also receiving blessings. You love a cheerful giver! You notice true generosity, and You reward it abundantly. . . .

PRAYER REQUESTS

PRAISES

ANSWERS TO PRAYER

SATURDAY, SEPTEMBER 21

"You parents—if your children ask for a loaf of bread, do you give them a stone instead? Or if they ask for a fish, do you give them a snake? Of course not! So if you sinful people know how to give good gifts to your children, how much more will your heavenly Father give good gifts to those who ask him."

MATTHEW 7:9–11 NLT

You are so loving and kind, heavenly Father! I trust that You enjoy giving me good gifts, and I'm so grateful for each and every blessing from You. . . .

PRAYER REQUESTS

ANSWERS TO PRAYER

PRAISES

SUNDAY, SEPTEMBER 22

First Day of Autumn

"While the earth lasts, planting time and gathering time, cold and heat, summer and winter, and day and night will not end."

GENESIS 8:22 NLV

Creator God, thank You for the gift of seasons of nature on the earth. There are beautiful blessings in each one. Help me to realize that my life is full of seasons too. The good times will not last forever but neither will the difficult ones. Please teach me and bless me and draw me closer to You through them all. . . .

PRAYER REQUESTS

PRAISES

ANSWERS TO PRAYER

MONDAY, SEPTEMBER 23

*Be filled with the Holy Spirit, singing psalms and hymns
and spiritual songs among yourselves, and making music
to the Lord in your hearts. And give thanks for everything
to God the Father in the name of our Lord Jesus Christ.*

EPHESIANS 5:18–20 NLT

Lord, thank You for the gift of music! I'm amazed by the creativity and musical ability You've given to Your people. Music brings me so much joy, especially when I'm singing praises to You. . . .

PRAYER REQUESTS

ANSWERS
TO PRAYER

PRAISES

TUESDAY, SEPTEMBER 24

"For I am the Lord your God Who holds your right hand,
and Who says to you, 'Do not be afraid. I will help you.'"
ISAIAH 41:13 NLV

I can't even fully wrap my mind around what an amazing blessing it is that You, almighty God, care for Your people so much that You hold us by the hand, promising to help us. I am grateful for Your presence and Your protection and Your care. . . .

PRAYER REQUESTS

PRAISES

ANSWERS TO PRAYER

WEDNESDAY, SEPTEMBER 25

*For God is working in you, giving you the
desire and the power to do what pleases him.*
PHILIPPIANS 2:13 NLT

Heavenly Father, thank You for working in me—for using my life and the gifts and talents You've given me to do the good things You've planned for me. With each new day, please align what I want with what You want. I'm so blessed to be able to do Your will. . . .

PRAYER REQUESTS

ANSWERS TO PRAYER

PRAISES

THURSDAY, SEPTEMBER 26

For the word of God is alive and powerful. It is sharper than the sharpest two-edged sword, cutting between soul and spirit, between joint and marrow. It exposes our innermost thoughts and desires.

HEBREWS 4:12 NLT

God, thank You for Your living and powerful Word! Help me to love hearing from You through it. Please continue to guide me and correct me with it as I seek You daily. Draw me closer and closer to You. . . .

PRAYER REQUESTS

PRAISES

ANSWERS TO PRAYER

FRIDAY, SEPTEMBER 27

"God opposes the proud but shows favor to the humble."
Humble yourselves, therefore, under God's mighty
hand, that he may lift you up in due time.

1 Peter 5:5–6 NIV

It's so easy to let my pride take over; so please, God, remind me every day that You oppose the proud and show favor to the humble. Lift me up and bless me in the ways You want to—in the ways that are best for me according to Your perfect knowledge and plans, not mine. . . .

PRAYER REQUESTS

ANSWERS
TO PRAYER

PRAISES

SATURDAY, SEPTEMBER 28

*Obey your spiritual leaders, and do what they say. Their work
is to watch over your souls, and they are accountable to God.
Give them reason to do this with joy and not with sorrow.*
HEBREWS 13:17 NLT

Lord, thank You so much for spiritual leaders whom You have called to preach
and teach Your Word. Please grow and mature me through their ministry. Help
me to respect and encourage them in their good work. . . .

PRAYER REQUESTS

PRAISES

ANSWERS TO PRAYER

SUNDAY, SEPTEMBER 29

Now all glory to God, who is able, through his mighty power at work within us, to accomplish infinitely more than we might ask or think. Glory to him in the church and in Christ Jesus through all generations forever and ever!

EPHESIANS 3:20–21 NLT

God, even as I ask You for blessings and receive them, I know my mind can't even fathom all the amazing things You can do above and beyond what I ask. I praise and thank You for all that You do and are going to do! . . .

PRAYER REQUESTS

ANSWERS TO PRAYER

PRAISES

MONDAY, SEPTEMBER 30

"No eye has seen, no ear has heard, and no mind has imagined what God has prepared for those who love him."

1 CORINTHIANS 2:9 NLT

Father, I believe that my very best blessings here on earth are just the slightest glimpse of all the good things You are preparing for those who love You. Those things are yet to come. Meanwhile, I delight in the blessings You have given me now. . . .

PRAYER REQUESTS

PRAISES

ANSWERS TO PRAYER

October

LIVING A COURAGEOUS LIFE

"You will receive power when the Holy Spirit comes into your life."

ACTS 1:8 NLV

SUNDAY	MONDAY	TUESDAY	WEDNESDAY	THURSDAY	FRIDAY	SATURDAY
		1	2	3	4	5
6	7	8	9	10	11	12
13	14	15	16	17	18	19
20	21 Columbus Day	22	23	24	25	26
27	28	29	30	31 Halloween		

When you became a Christian, the Holy Spirit took up residence inside your heart. That's the same power that raised Jesus from the dead (Ephesians 1:19–20). The Spirit is your comforter, counselor, and encourager. You can have courage in any challenge because He is there to help you. He will not leave you to fend for yourself. Fear not!

TUESDAY, OCTOBER 1

God has not given us a spirit of fear and timidity,
but of power, love, and self-discipline.
2 TIMOTHY 1:7 NLT

Father, when I am intimidated by circumstances or people, remind me that You created me in Your image. Your Spirit inside me gives me courage to live boldly in love. Help me to stand up for what's right, no matter what the cost. May I always act and react in kindness, in a way that honors You and gives all glory to You. . . .

PRAYER REQUESTS

PRAISES

ANSWERS TO PRAYER

WEDNESDAY, OCTOBER 2

I can do all things because Christ gives me the strength.
Philippians 4:13 NLV

I get overwhelmed by difficult things sometimes, Lord. On days when challenges feel especially frustrating, remind me that You are beside me and will give me the strength I need to do hard things, to do impossible things, to do *all* things. And after Your strength pulls me through, I will stop and praise You because You are faithful to come through in every situation! . . .

PRAYER REQUESTS

ANSWERS
TO PRAYER

PRAISES

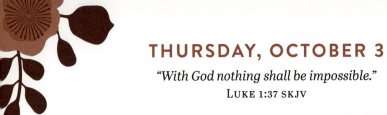

THURSDAY, OCTOBER 3

"With God nothing shall be impossible."
LUKE 1:37 SKJV

Father, I am thankful that You can do *anything*! There is nothing that can stop You. No force of nature, no human plan, no evil scheme, not even Satan himself can keep You from completing Your will. I choose to come alongside Your plan. Use me as You want to, because I know whatever You are doing, I want to be a part of it now and forever. . . .

PRAYER REQUESTS

PRAISES

ANSWERS TO PRAYER

FRIDAY, OCTOBER 4

Truly he is my rock and my salvation;
he is my fortress, I will never be shaken.
PSALM 62:2 NIV

When the world makes me anxious and fearful, help me remember to run to You, Father. You cannot and will not be shaken by any problem, frustration, trauma, or failure. I am always welcome in Your presence, and You are a fortress against everything that scares me. Here I will find rest and contentment. . . .

PRAYER REQUESTS

ANSWERS TO PRAYER

PRAISES

SATURDAY, OCTOBER 5

"This is my command—be strong and courageous! Do not be afraid or discouraged. For the LORD your God is with you wherever you go."
JOSHUA 1:9 NLT

I want to live fearlessly for You, Lord. But sometimes, I don't feel strong and courageous. Sometimes I feel weak and anxious. When these feelings arise, make Your presence known, Father. Show up in a big way, and I will look up and see Your face. I will hear Your encouraging words and move ahead in confidence. . . .

PRAYER REQUESTS

PRAISES

ANSWERS TO PRAYER

SUNDAY, OCTOBER 6

Let us then with confidence draw near to the throne of grace,
that we may receive mercy and find grace to help in time of need.
HEBREWS 4:16 ESV

When I am feeling empty and far from You, God, give me the confidence to approach You. You are not angry with me; You are not disappointed in me. You want to shower me with mercy and grace—to refresh me and fill my heart with Your Spirit so I can shine Your light to others. . . .

PRAYER REQUESTS

ANSWERS TO PRAYER

PRAISES

MONDAY, OCTOBER 7

The earnest prayer of a righteous person has great power and produces wonderful results.
JAMES 5:16 NLT

Today I am choosing prayer as a first option rather than a last resort, Father. I will be faithful to earnestly ask, seek, and knock. As my prayer life grows and deepens my relationship with You, please move powerfully in my life. I am eagerly awaiting the wonderful results of my prayers, because I know I am already blessed by spending time with You. . . .

PRAYER REQUESTS

PRAISES

ANSWERS TO PRAYER

TUESDAY, OCTOBER 8

He gives power to the faint, and He increases
the strength of those who have no might.
ISAIAH 40:29 SKJV

Some days I am weak, Lord. I feel zapped of energy and strength of heart. On those days, please give me an extra portion of Your power. And when I see others around me struggling, help me share Your might with them as well. Strengthen us together in You, and we will give You all the praise because we know we couldn't do it on our own. . . .

PRAYER REQUESTS

ANSWERS
TO PRAYER

PRAISES

WEDNESDAY, OCTOBER 9

*The name of the L**ORD** is a fortified tower;*
the righteous run to it and are safe.

PROVERBS 18:10 NIV

Father God, raise me to Your level, above the daily frustrations of the world. Help me to keep my mind on the details that really matter: loving You and loving others. Keep me focused on eternal things, like building Your kingdom here and now. Guard my heart in the safety of Your tower, Lord. . . .

PRAYER REQUESTS

PRAISES

ANSWERS TO PRAYER

THURSDAY, OCTOBER 10

When I called, you answered me;
you greatly emboldened me.
PSALM 138:3 NIV

You are faithful to hear my prayers, almighty God. That fact alone encourages me. But Your Word tells me that when I call to You, You will answer me. And that fact gives me courage to step forward in my faith on my journey through life. Thank You for always providing the strength, peace, hope, and grace that I need every day. I love You, Lord. . . .

PRAYER REQUESTS

ANSWERS
TO PRAYER

PRAISES

FRIDAY, OCTOBER 11

For the word of God is alive and powerful. It is sharper than the sharpest two-edged sword, cutting between soul and spirit, between joint and marrow. It exposes our innermost thoughts and desires.

HEBREWS 4:12 NLT

Thank You for the blessing of the Bible, Father. Although it was written thousands of years ago, Your Word speaks to me today with encouragement and challenge and provides me with perspective. Reading it, I learn more about You and my faith grows stronger. . . .

PRAYER REQUESTS

PRAISES

ANSWERS TO PRAYER

SATURDAY, OCTOBER 12

*Elijah was as human as we are, and yet when he prayed earnestly
that no rain would fall, none fell for three and a half years!*
JAMES 5:17 NLT

I will not set a limit on what prayer can do, Lord, because I know You are the source
of power behind the prayer. Make my heart in tune with Your will, Father, so that
my prayers can be as effective as Elijah's prayers. Show Your might through my
prayers so I can show others how You are working in my life. . . .

PRAYER REQUESTS

ANSWERS
TO PRAYER

PRAISES

SUNDAY, OCTOBER 13

"Don't be afraid; just believe."
MARK 5:36 NIV

When fear creeps its way into my life, Jesus, help me to turn away from the things that make me anxious and to hold tighter to my faith. I believe You lived on earth fully God and fully human. I believe You died and rose again. I believe Your sacrifice covers my sins. I believe I will live forever with You in the presence of our heavenly Father. These promises give me hope and courage. . . .

PRAYER REQUESTS

PRAISES

ANSWERS TO PRAYER

MONDAY, OCTOBER 14

Columbus Day

Therefore put on the full armor of God, so that when the day of evil comes, you may be able to stand your ground, and after you have done everything, to stand.

EPHESIANS 6:13 NIV

God, even though evil will come when I least expect it, I will not live in fear. I will prepare myself every day with the protection of Your armor. Truth, righteousness, faith, peace, and the Holy Spirit are all I need to stand firm no matter what comes my way. . . .

PRAYER REQUESTS

ANSWERS TO PRAYER

PRAISES

TUESDAY, OCTOBER 15

Stand firm then, with the belt of truth buckled around
your waist, with the breastplate of righteousness in place.
EPHESIANS 6:14 NIV

The world constantly questions truth, God. But I let Your truth be the test of what is good and real. I will keep Your truth firmly around me, and I will shine the light of truth in this confused world. Keep Your righteousness near me, encouraging me to stand for right, no matter the cost. . . .

PRAYER REQUESTS

PRAISES

ANSWERS TO PRAYER

WEDNESDAY, OCTOBER 16

For shoes, put on the peace that comes from the
Good News so that you will be fully prepared.
EPHESIANS 6:15 NLT

Make me a peacemaker, Lord. When there is fighting and turmoil around me, may the good news of Jesus' love always be on my lips. Help me to build strong relationships with others so they can trust me to offer a listening ear and a shoulder to lean on. Prepare me and use me, Lord, as You want to. . . .

PRAYER REQUESTS

ANSWERS TO PRAYER

PRAISES

THURSDAY, OCTOBER 17

*In addition to all of these, hold up the shield of faith to stop
the fiery arrows of the devil. Put on salvation as your helmet,
and take the sword of the Spirit, which is the word of God.*
EPHESIANS 6:16–17 NLT

Lord, when I am attacked, my faith in You helps me remain assured of Your protection and rescue. I believe in the permanence of my salvation through Your grace, and I am encouraged and refreshed by Your Word, the Bible. . . .

PRAYER REQUESTS

PRAISES

ANSWERS TO PRAYER

FRIDAY, OCTOBER 18

They do not fear bad news; they confidently
trust the Lord to care for them.
Psalm 112:7 nlt

I refuse to live in fear of bad news, Lord, because a life controlled by fear is not the life of freedom You offer. Instead, I will live in the hope that You will take care of any problems that come my way. I believe You are faithful to make all things (good *or* bad) work together for my good (Romans 8:28). . . .

PRAYER REQUESTS

ANSWERS
TO PRAYER

PRAISES

SATURDAY, OCTOBER 19

"Don't be afraid, for I am with you. Don't be discouraged,
for I am your God. I will strengthen you and help you.
I will hold you up with my victorious right hand."
ISAIAH 41:10 NLT

Almighty God, You tell me not to be afraid because You are with me. You tell me not to be discouraged, and You promise to give me strength and to help me and hold me up. Because of these beautiful promises, I have hope. I will not fear. . . .

PRAYER REQUESTS

PRAISES

ANSWERS TO PRAYER

SUNDAY, OCTOBER 20

God is faithful. He will not allow you to be tempted more than you can take. But when you are tempted, He will make a way for you to keep from falling into sin.
1 CORINTHIANS 10:13 NLV

Temptations exist around every corner, Father. But I know You are faithful to provide a way out. I can avoid sin when I am tempted to do something outside Your will. Give me the wisdom to steer clear of the situations where I struggle the most. . . .

PRAYER REQUESTS

ANSWERS TO PRAYER

PRAISES

MONDAY, OCTOBER 21

Don't be intimidated in any way by your enemies. This will
be a sign to them that they are going to be destroyed,
but that you are going to be saved, even by God himself.
PHILIPPIANS 1:28 NLT

I need Your help, mighty God, to firmly stand up to those who mean to do me harm. I will not be intimidated by them, because You are on my side. Help me speak Your truth in love in every situation, and I know I will prevail. . . .

PRAYER REQUESTS

PRAISES

ANSWERS TO PRAYER

TUESDAY, OCTOBER 22

*I know the L*ORD *is always with me. I will
not be shaken, for he is right beside me.*
PSALM 16:8 NLT

Father, help me to understand, like the writer of Psalm 16 understood, that You are always with me. That doesn't mean that You are with me in some vague, metaphorical sense; it means You are here, now, right beside me. Even though I can't physically touch You, I believe the promise that You are here. And because of that, nothing will rattle me. . . .

PRAYER REQUESTS

ANSWERS
TO PRAYER

PRAISES

WEDNESDAY, OCTOBER 23

The Lord is my light and my salvation. Whom shall I fear?
The Lord is the strength of my life. Of whom shall I be afraid?
PSALM 27:1 SKJV

I may not be afraid of the dark like I was as a child, Lord, but sometimes the darkness is unnerving. When my life feels dark and I can't see what dangers surround me, be my constant source of light and strength. I know that You have saved me and that I have no reason to fear. . . .

PRAYER REQUESTS

PRAISES

ANSWERS TO PRAYER

THURSDAY, OCTOBER 24

I trust in God, so why should I be afraid?
What can mere mortals do to me?
PSALM 56:4 NLT

When I feel intimidated by people or situations or the unknown, Lord, give me a correct perspective. You are so much bigger than any threat I may experience. You are the Creator of all, and You control everything that happens in Your creation. I trust that You want what's best for me. I have faith that You will deliver on all Your promises, so please take away my fears. . . .

PRAYER REQUESTS

ANSWERS TO PRAYER

PRAISES

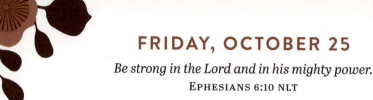

FRIDAY, OCTOBER 25

Be strong in the Lord and in his mighty power.
EPHESIANS 6:10 NLT

Although the world tells me that I am capable, self-sufficient, and strong, Father, I know the truth is that I am only those things because You make me so. It is *Your* strength that makes me strong. It is *Your* power that sustains me. Thank You for allowing me to share in Your awesome might, and help me to encourage others with Your greatness. . . .

PRAYER REQUESTS

PRAISES

ANSWERS TO PRAYER

SATURDAY, OCTOBER 26

"If we are thrown into the blazing furnace, the God we serve is able to deliver us from it, and he will deliver us from Your Majesty's hand. But even if he does not, we want you to know, Your Majesty, that we will not serve your gods or worship the image of gold you have set up."

DANIEL 3:17–18 NIV

Give me the faith of Shadrach, Meshach, and Abednego, Lord. Give me confidence so I will believe that You will rescue me from anything. . . .

PRAYER REQUESTS

ANSWERS TO PRAYER

PRAISES

SUNDAY, OCTOBER 27

Jesus said, "Come!" Peter got out of the
boat and walked on the water to Jesus.
MATTHEW 14:29 NLV

When You invite me to step out in faith, Jesus, give me the courage to follow You anywhere. Even when fear of the unknown surrounds me, even when it looks like my footing is as dangerous as walking on water, reassure me of Your presence and protection. I know I will find freedom, safety, and peace wherever You are.

PRAYER REQUESTS

PRAISES

ANSWERS TO PRAYER

MONDAY, OCTOBER 28

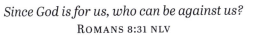

Since God is for us, who can be against us?
ROMANS 8:31 NLV

Even if it seems like the entire world is against me, God, remind me of the truth that You are for me. You are on my side—in my corner—giving me the strength to stand for truth. And when I can't manage to fight, You fight for me. I refuse to live in a piteous, "poor me" state; because You and I are on the same team, I am victorious! . . .

PRAYER REQUESTS

ANSWERS TO PRAYER

PRAISES

TUESDAY, OCTOBER 29

*There is no fear in love. But perfect love drives
out fear, because fear has to do with punishment.
The one who fears is not made perfect in love.*

1 JOHN 4:18 NIV

Father, I know in my head and heart that You love me. Yet worry still has a way of creeping into my life. So, today, I am giving You my fears and asking for Your perfect love to cover me with the confidence of Your mercy and grace. . . .

PRAYER REQUESTS

PRAISES

ANSWERS TO PRAYER

WEDNESDAY, OCTOBER 30

*Joseph of Arimathea took a risk and went
to Pilate and asked for Jesus' body.*
MARK 15:43 NLT

What other people may see as a risk I see as direction from You, Lord. Give me understanding of Your perfect will so I can further Your kingdom like Joseph of Arimathea did. If I hesitate, assure me that I'm acting according to Your plan. And when great things result, I will give all glory to You! You are the God of miracles! . . .

PRAYER REQUESTS

ANSWERS TO PRAYER

PRAISES

THURSDAY, OCTOBER 31

Halloween

"Who knows if you have not become queen for such a time as this?"
ESTHER 4:14 NLV

You have made me for a unique purpose, Father God. And just like Esther, You brought me to this time in history, to this place, among specific friends and family. Today, I'm asking You to reveal Your individual plan for me. Please mold my thoughts, words, and actions to be Yours. Help me see the world through Your eyes so I can be Your hands and feet. . . .

PRAYER REQUESTS

PRAISES

ANSWERS TO PRAYER

November

CONTENTMENT AND GRATITUDE

I have learned in whatever situation I am to be content....
I can do all things through him who strengthens me.
PHILIPPIANS 4:11, 13 ESV

SUNDAY	MONDAY	TUESDAY	WEDNESDAY	THURSDAY	FRIDAY	SATURDAY
					1	2
3	4	5	6	7	8	9
Daylight Saving Time Ends 10	11	Election Day 12	13	14	15	16
17	Veterans Day 18	19	20	21	22	23
24	25	26	27	28 Thanksgiving	29	30

The apostle Paul taught the secret to contentment—that in every situation and circumstance, no matter how high or low, we can do anything and everything through Jesus Christ, who strengthens us. We can enjoy in times of plenty, and we can endure in times of need. God is sovereign, and He is caring for us through it all.

FRIDAY, NOVEMBER 1

"Give us today our daily bread."
MATTHEW 6:11 NIV

Jesus, when You gave us an example of how to pray, You showed us that we should ask to have enough food for the day. Help me to be grateful and content with my needs being met at present and not worried about how they will be met in the future. I trust You will always provide for me. . . .

PRAYER REQUESTS

PRAISES

ANSWERS TO PRAYER

SATURDAY, NOVEMBER 2

"So do not worry, saying, 'What shall we eat?' or 'What shall we drink?' or 'What shall we wear?' For the pagans run after all these things, and your heavenly Father knows that you need them. But seek first his kingdom and his righteousness, and all these things will be given to you as well."

MATTHEW 6:31–33 NIV

Heavenly Father, help me to be focused on seeking You and Your will first of all—trusting that everything else falls into place after that. . . .

PRAYER REQUESTS

ANSWERS TO PRAYER

PRAISES

SUNDAY, NOVEMBER 3

Daylight Saving Time Ends

And we know that God causes everything to work together for the good of those who love God and are called according to his purpose for them.

ROMANS 8:28 NLT

Heavenly Father, no matter the season or situation I'm in, I believe this scripture. I trust that You are working the blessings and the hardships, the joy and the pain all together for good. I love You always! Please continue to guide me in the purposes and plans You have for me. . . .

PRAYER REQUESTS

PRAISES

ANSWERS TO PRAYER

MONDAY, NOVEMBER 4

You, O Lord, are a covering around me, my shining-greatness, and the One Who lifts my head. I was crying to the Lord with my voice. And He answered me from His holy mountain. I lay down and slept, and I woke up again, for the Lord keeps me safe.

PSALM 3:3–5 NLV

Heavenly Father, I'm so grateful You let me cry everything out to You. And then You lift my head again with loving care. I can face anything with You as my constant source of help and hope. . . .

PRAYER REQUESTS

ANSWERS TO PRAYER

PRAISES

TUESDAY, NOVEMBER 5
Election Day

"Praise the name of God forever and ever, for he has all wisdom and power. He controls the course of world events; he removes kings and sets up other kings. He gives wisdom to the wise and knowledge to the scholars."
DANIEL 2:20–21 NLT

Lord, I believe that nothing is going on in the world that You don't have ultimate control over. And so I can have contentment and peace no matter what I hear in the news. I'm grateful for You, and I praise Your name forever. . . .

PRAYER REQUESTS

PRAISES

ANSWERS TO PRAYER

WEDNESDAY, NOVEMBER 6

"Don't store up treasures here on earth, where moths eat them and rust destroys them, and where thieves break in and steal. Store your treasures in heaven, where moths and rust cannot destroy, and thieves do not break in and steal. Wherever your treasure is, there the desires of your heart will also be."

MATTHEW 6:19–21 NLT

Lord, I want to be content with my life in the world, knowing that heaven is where the real rewards are. This life is fleeting. Life in Your presence will be forever. Until then, please guide me in all the good things You want me to do in the time You've given me here on earth. . . .

PRAYER REQUESTS

ANSWERS
TO PRAYER

PRAISES

THURSDAY, NOVEMBER 7

"You keep him in perfect peace whose mind is stayed on you, because he trusts in you. Trust in the Lord forever, for the Lord God is an everlasting rock."
ISAIAH 26:3–4 ESV

Lord God, I'm so grateful that You are my everlasting rock, worthy of all my trust forever. Thank You for giving me perfect peace as I keep my mind fixed on You. . . .

PRAYER REQUESTS

PRAISES

ANSWERS TO PRAYER

FRIDAY, NOVEMBER 8

Keep your life free from love of money, and be content with what you have, for he has said, "I will never leave you nor forsake you."
HEBREWS 13:5 ESV

Lord, please help me to be careful in my mindset about money. It's easy to get caught up in thinking more money means more security and happiness. But that's not true. And Your Word says not to love money but to be content with whatever I have. I always have You with me, and You provide everything I need....

PRAYER REQUESTS

ANSWERS TO PRAYER

PRAISES

SATURDAY, NOVEMBER 9

Trust in the LORD with all your heart; do not depend on your own understanding. Seek his will in all you do, and he will show you which path to take.

PROVERBS 3:5–6 NLT

Lord, please help me be content to not depend on my own understanding, because I admit—I sometimes do not understand You and Your ways at all. Despite that, I never want to stop trusting in You. Even when I'm feeling uncertain, please keep me step by step on the paths You have planned for me. More than anything else, I long to do Your will. . . .

PRAYER REQUESTS

PRAISES

ANSWERS TO PRAYER

SUNDAY, NOVEMBER 10

Better to have little, with godliness, than to be rich and dishonest.
PROVERBS 16:8 NLT

Lord, I don't want to forget this proverb. It's always better to have little of the things of this world and be full of Your love and peace than to be rich in the things of this world but poor in knowledge of and relationship with You. Help me to be consistent in living out that truth, and help me to share that truth with others. . . .

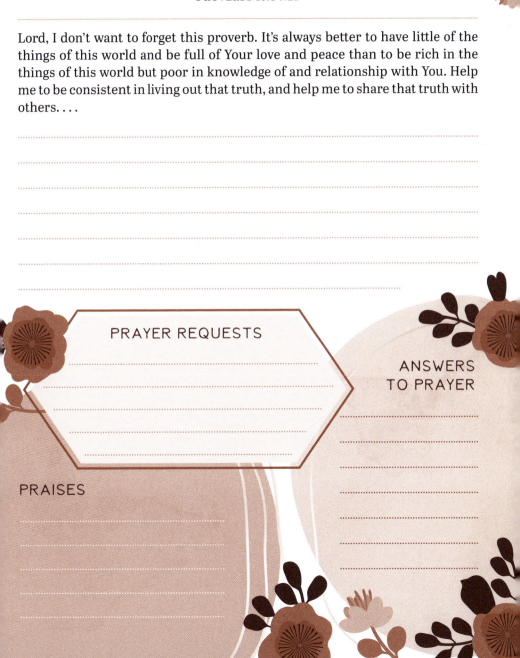

PRAYER REQUESTS

ANSWERS TO PRAYER

PRAISES

MONDAY, NOVEMBER 11
Veterans Day

*"My command is this: Love each other as I have
loved you. Greater love has no one than this:
to lay down one's life for one's friends."*

JOHN 15:12–13 NIV

Jesus, there aren't enough words in all the world to thank You for laying down Your life to save us from sin. Thank You for Your example of sacrifice. And thank You for those who give up their lives today through service to our country, to protect our nation and its citizens and our freedom to worship You. . . .

PRAYER REQUESTS

PRAISES

ANSWERS TO PRAYER

TUESDAY, NOVEMBER 12

*Greed causes fighting; trusting the L*ORD *leads to prosperity.*
PROVERBS 28:25 NLT

I have seen the truth of this proverb time and time again in the world, Lord. And I'm not proud to say I've seen it in my own life too. Forgive me when I am greedy, and please help me to be more and more content every day with whatever blessings You decide to give me—trusting fully that all true prosperity is found in a relationship with You. . . .

PRAYER REQUESTS

ANSWERS TO PRAYER

PRAISES

WEDNESDAY, NOVEMBER 13

He said to me, "My grace is sufficient for you, for my power is made perfect in weakness." Therefore I will boast all the more gladly of my weaknesses, so that the power of Christ may rest upon me. For the sake of Christ, then, I am content with weaknesses, insults, hardships, persecutions, and calamities. For when I am weak, then I am strong.

2 CORINTHIANS 12:9–10 ESV

Jesus, I want to be content in the midst of hard things, because I remember that my weakness makes me depend on You all the more—and that is the greatest gift. . . .

PRAYER REQUESTS

PRAISES

ANSWERS TO PRAYER

THURSDAY, NOVEMBER 14

The Lord is my Shepherd. I will have everything I need. He lets me rest in fields of green grass. He leads me beside the quiet waters. He makes me strong again. He leads me in the way of living right with Himself which brings honor to His name. Yes, even if I walk through the valley of the shadow of death, I will not be afraid of anything, because You are with me.

PSALM 23:1–4 NLV

Your Word is so soothing, Lord! Thank You for being my Good Shepherd and providing me with everything I need. . . .

PRAYER REQUESTS

ANSWERS TO PRAYER

PRAISES

FRIDAY, NOVEMBER 15

A God-like life gives us much when we are happy for what we have. We came into this world with nothing. For sure, when we die, we will take nothing with us. If we have food and clothing, let us be happy. But men who want lots of money are tempted. They are trapped into doing all kinds of foolish things and things which hurt them. These things drag them into sin and will destroy them.

1 TIMOTHY 6:6–9 NLV

Lord, help me to never forget the warnings in this scripture. I want to be happy always with whatever You see fit to bless me with. . . .

PRAYER REQUESTS

PRAISES

ANSWERS TO PRAYER

SATURDAY, NOVEMBER 16

God has given us everything we need for living a godly life. We have received all of this by coming to know him, the one who called us to himself by means of his marvelous glory and excellence. And because of his glory and excellence, he has given us great and precious promises. These are the promises that enable you to share his divine nature and escape the world's corruption caused by human desires.

2 PETER 1:3–4 NLT

God, I'm so grateful You have given me everything I need to live a godly life. Thank You that because of Your great power and love for me, I can escape the world's corruption. . . .

PRAYER REQUESTS

ANSWERS TO PRAYER

PRAISES

SUNDAY, NOVEMBER 17

Where can I go from Your Spirit? Or where can I run away from where You are? If I go up to heaven, You are there! If I make my bed in the place of the dead, You are there! If I take the wings of the morning or live in the farthest part of the sea, even there Your hand will lead me and Your right hand will hold me.

PSALM 139:7–10 NLV

It's so reassuring to know that You are absolutely everywhere, Lord. Thank You for leading me, holding me, and helping me in every place and every situation. . . .

PRAYER REQUESTS

PRAISES

ANSWERS TO PRAYER

MONDAY, NOVEMBER 18

Therefore we do not lose heart. Though outwardly we are wasting away, yet inwardly we are being renewed day by day. For our light and momentary troubles are achieving for us an eternal glory that far outweighs them all. So we fix our eyes not on what is seen, but on what is unseen, since what is seen is temporary, but what is unseen is eternal.

2 Corinthians 4:16–18 NIV

This life of mine and this world are only temporary. Thank You for helping me to never lose heart, Lord, as I fix my eyes on You. . . .

PRAYER REQUESTS

ANSWERS TO PRAYER

PRAISES

TUESDAY, NOVEMBER 19

Put on the full armor of God, so that when the day of evil comes, you may be able to stand your ground. . . . Stand firm then, with the belt of truth buckled around your waist, with the breastplate of righteousness in place, and with your feet fitted with the readiness that comes from the gospel of peace. In addition to all this, take up the shield of faith, with which you can extinguish all the flaming arrows of the evil one. Take the helmet of salvation and the sword of the Spirit, which is the word of God.

EPHESIANS 6:13–17 NIV

Thank You, God, for protecting me and equipping me to stand strong against evil. . . .

PRAYER REQUESTS

PRAISES

ANSWERS TO PRAYER

WEDNESDAY, NOVEMBER 20

*"Watch out! Be on your guard against all kinds of greed;
life does not consist in an abundance of possessions."*
LUKE 12:15 NIV

Jesus, it's so easy to look around at the lives of others and want what they have rather than to simply be content with my own life and blessings. So, please help me to watch out and be on guard against comparison and greed. You love and want to protect me, and I want to remember Your good warnings. . . .

PRAYER REQUESTS

ANSWERS
TO PRAYER

PRAISES

THURSDAY, NOVEMBER 21

His loving-kindness for those who fear Him is as great as the heavens are high above the earth. He has taken our sins from us as far as the east is from the west. The Lord has loving-pity on those who fear Him, as a father has loving-pity on his children.

PSALM 103:11–13 NLV

Lord, I'm beyond grateful for Your generous love and grace and mercy. Thank You for taking my sins far away from me. . . .

PRAYER REQUESTS

PRAISES

ANSWERS TO PRAYER

FRIDAY, NOVEMBER 22

How sweet is Your Word to my taste! It is sweeter than honey to my mouth! I get understanding from Your Law and so I hate every false way. Your Word is a lamp to my feet and a light to my path.

PSALM 119:103–105 NLV

Lord, I need Your Word to light my path and guide me every day. It is so good, and I'm so grateful for it. Help me to love and crave more of Your Word every day. . . .

PRAYER REQUESTS

ANSWERS TO PRAYER

PRAISES

SATURDAY, NOVEMBER 23

*Therefore, since we are receiving a kingdom that
cannot be shaken, let us be thankful, and so worship
God acceptably with reverence and awe.*
HEBREWS 12:28 NIV

Lord, the world feels shaky, and so do my personal circumstances at times. So I'm grateful that nothing can shake Your kingdom. Remind me of this truth, especially when life gets chaotic. You are holy and just, and You are sovereign over everything. Nothing can stop You and Your perfect plans. . . .

PRAYER REQUESTS

PRAISES

ANSWERS TO PRAYER

SUNDAY, NOVEMBER 24

God has said, "I will never leave you or let you be
alone." So we can say for sure, "The Lord is my Helper.
I am not afraid of anything man can do to me."
HEBREWS 13:5–6 NLV

Where would I be without You as my helper, Lord? I can't thank You enough for never leaving me alone. Remind me that I never need to be afraid of anything because of Your constant presence with me. . . .

PRAYER REQUESTS

ANSWERS TO PRAYER

PRAISES

MONDAY, NOVEMBER 25

Are not all the angels spirits who work for God? They are sent out to help those who are to be saved from the punishment of sin.
HEBREWS 1:14 NLV

Heavenly Father, thank You that angels are real. I'm so grateful You send them out to help me when I need it. Thank You for the ways You have cared for me and protected me through the work of angels in the past—and for all the ways I trust You will in the future too. . . .

PRAYER REQUESTS

PRAISES

ANSWERS TO PRAYER

TUESDAY, NOVEMBER 26

We want you to know for sure about those who have died. You have no reason to have sorrow as those who have no hope. We believe that Jesus died and then came to life again. Because we believe this, we know that God will bring to life again all those who belong to Jesus.

1 THESSALONIANS 4:13–14 NLV

Thank You, Jesus, for the wonderful peace and contentment of knowing that I will see again my loved ones who have died but who trusted You as Savior. You give eternal life to all who belong to You! . . .

PRAYER REQUESTS

ANSWERS TO PRAYER

PRAISES

WEDNESDAY, NOVEMBER 27

Surely goodness and mercy shall follow me all the days of
my life, and I will dwell in the house of the LORD forever.
PSALM 23:6 SKJV

Heavenly Father, help me to notice and appreciate each and every bit of goodness and mercy You are constantly giving me, even in the midst of trials. I praise You and thank You for it all, and I trust in You to continue to give it. . . .

PRAYER REQUESTS

PRAISES

ANSWERS TO PRAYER

THURSDAY, NOVEMBER 28

Thanksgiving

*Rejoice always. Pray without ceasing. Give thanks in everything,
for this is the will of God in Christ Jesus concerning you.*

1 THESSALONIANS 5:16–18 SKJV

Lord, I want my mind to be focused on You—with rejoicing, prayer, and gratitude—not just here and there throughout my days but constantly. I want to look for Your blessings, both big and small, in every moment, and to praise and thank You for them. Help me to rid my mind of negativity and anything that distracts me from You. . . .

PRAYER REQUESTS

ANSWERS
TO PRAYER

PRAISES

FRIDAY, NOVEMBER 29

Give all your cares to the Lord and He will give you strength. He will never let those who are right with Him be shaken. But You, O God, will bring the sinful down into the hole that destroys. Men who kill and lie will not live out half their days. But I will trust in You.

PSALM 55:22–23 NLV

Heavenly Father, thank You so much that You tell me time and again to give my worries and cares to You. You want to replace them with Your perfect peace and strength, and I'm so grateful. . . .

PRAYER REQUESTS

PRAISES

ANSWERS TO PRAYER

SATURDAY, NOVEMBER 30

But as for me, I trust in You, O Lord. I say,
"You are my God." My times are in Your hands.
PSALM 31:14–15 NLV

Heavenly Father, in any situation, good or bad, I want to remember and repeat the simple but powerful words of this psalm. Fill me with gratitude, contentment, and peace because I trust in You, You are my God, and my times are in Your hands. . . .

PRAYER REQUESTS

ANSWERS TO PRAYER

PRAISES

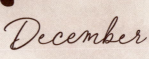

December

WHEN GOD SAYS "WAIT"

They who wait upon the Lord will get new strength.
They will rise up with wings like eagles. They will run
and not get tired. They will walk and not become weak.

ISAIAH 40:31 NLV

SUNDAY	MONDAY	TUESDAY	WEDNESDAY	THURSDAY	FRIDAY	SATURDAY
1	2	3	4	5	6	7
8	9	10	11	12	13	14
15	16	17	18	19	20	21 First Day of Winter
22	23	24 Christmas Eve	25 Christmas Day Hanukkah Begins at Sundown	26	27	28
29	30	31 New Year's Eve				

Advent is a season of waiting for the arrival of the promised Messiah. What are you waiting for today? Ask God for strength while you wait in hopeful anticipation of His answer. He will bless you in the waiting.

SUNDAY, DECEMBER 1

God has made everything beautiful for its own time. He has planted eternity in the human heart, but even so, people cannot see the whole scope of God's work from beginning to end.

ECCLESIASTES 3:11 NLT

Today I am reminding myself that You are an eternal God. When I am impatient and don't understand why You aren't acting, help me to remember that You have created me to be eternal with You. Your timing is perfect, and You *are* working, Father. . . .

PRAYER REQUESTS

ANSWERS TO PRAYER

PRAISES

MONDAY, DECEMBER 2

For sure there is a future and your hope will not be cut off.

PROVERBS 23:18 NLV

What does my future hold, Lord? I wish I knew! I have so many dreams about what tomorrow could be for me and for the people I love. While I wait for tomorrow to come, I will put my hope in Your promises. Lead me forward, Lord, into Your future, and I know I will find peace and contentment forever....

PRAYER REQUESTS

PRAISES

ANSWERS TO PRAYER

TUESDAY, DECEMBER 3

*For all of God's promises have been fulfilled in Christ
with a resounding "Yes!" And through Christ, our "Amen"
(which means "Yes") ascends to God for his glory.*
2 CORINTHIANS 1:20 NLT

Father, You sent Your Son to earth as a baby, the long-awaited fulfillment of the promise of a Savior for Your people. Thank You for always being faithful in Your promises. You are a God I can count on no matter what! Even while I wait for answers to my own prayers, I take hope in Your faithfulness. . . .

PRAYER REQUESTS

ANSWERS TO PRAYER

PRAISES

WEDNESDAY, DECEMBER 4

*Be still before the L*ORD *and wait patiently for him;*
do not fret when people succeed in their ways,
when they carry out their wicked schemes.
PSALM 37:7 NIV

I admit I struggle with patience, Lord. But I know I am in Your will, and I will wait on Your timing. You are never early, and You are never late. You understand the whole picture of my life and how it fits into Your kingdom. Give me good work to do while I wait. . . .

PRAYER REQUESTS

PRAISES

ANSWERS TO PRAYER

THURSDAY, DECEMBER 5

*As for me, I look to the L*ORD *for help. I wait confidently for
God to save me, and my God will certainly hear me.*
MICAH 7:7 NLT

You are my Savior, Jesus. You have rescued me from death and given me eternal life, and You are faithful to save me from the thing I'm struggling with now. You are able to handle anything, big or small. What's more is that You *care* about and *listen* to me when I struggle. . . .

PRAYER REQUESTS

ANSWERS TO PRAYER

PRAISES

FRIDAY, DECEMBER 6

I am counting on the LORD; yes, I am counting on him. I have put my hope in his word.
PSALM 130:5 NLT

I've been burned by counting on people and things in this world, Lord. Letdowns and betrayals make it hard to trust. But today I am counting on You! I read in Your Word about Your fulfilled promises. So I ask You now, please show up soon. I believe You will. I need You. . . .

PRAYER REQUESTS

PRAISES

ANSWERS TO PRAYER

SATURDAY, DECEMBER 7

Let all that I am wait quietly before God,
for my hope is in him.
PSALM 62:5 NLT

There's a lot going on inside my head and heart these days, Father. My schedule is crazy, and it feels like I have such little time to sit quietly with You. But for this moment, I am focusing on You with everything in me. I breathe You in, feeling the life-giving power of the Holy Spirit well up. Thank You for the hope I have in You. . . .

PRAYER REQUESTS

ANSWERS TO PRAYER

PRAISES

SUNDAY, DECEMBER 8

O Lord, be kind to us. We have waited for You. Be our strength every morning. Save us in the time of trouble.
ISAIAH 33:2 NLV

Lord, please give me an extra dose of Your strength while I wait for You to answer my prayers. Remind me of Your loving-kindness and that You care about how I'm feeling in this season. I have waited and will continue to wait in hopeful expectation of Your miracles in my life. . . .

PRAYER REQUESTS

PRAISES

ANSWERS TO PRAYER

MONDAY, DECEMBER 9

We confidently and joyfully look forward to sharing God's glory. We can rejoice, too, when we run into problems and trials, for we know that they help us develop endurance.
ROMANS 5:2–3 NLT

I'm so used to instant gratification, Lord, that this season of developing endurance feels impossible some days. Rather than focusing on my struggles now, may I glimpse Your coming glory. I will be confident in the joy of knowing You are in control! . . .

PRAYER REQUESTS

ANSWERS TO PRAYER

PRAISES

TUESDAY, DECEMBER 10

*Be patient, then, brothers and sisters, until the Lord's coming.
See how the farmer waits for the land to yield its valuable
crop, patiently waiting for the autumn and spring rains.*
JAMES 5:7 NIV

In Your wonderful creation, You have set the timing for the four seasons. The new life of spring wouldn't be as beautiful and miraculous if it followed summer. While I wait for You, Lord, help me to see Your beauty and Your work all around me. . . .

PRAYER REQUESTS

PRAISES

ANSWERS TO PRAYER

WEDNESDAY, DECEMBER 11

I will praise you forever, O God, for what you have done.
PSALM 52:9 NLT

You have never failed me, God. Help me to remember that when I am waiting for You to answer my prayers. Thank You for the past victories You have given me. I praise You for the good test results, the restored relationships, the unexpected blessings, the resources that stretched further than they should've, the encouragement when I needed it most. You are faithful and true! . . .

PRAYER REQUESTS

ANSWERS TO PRAYER

PRAISES

THURSDAY, DECEMBER 12

*Let us not become weary in doing good, for at the
proper time we will reap a harvest if we do not give up.*
GALATIANS 6:9 NIV

Father, thank You for the opportunity to do good in the world. Channel my good deeds to be work that builds up Your kingdom. I want to shine Your light to everyone around me so that they will be attracted to Your glory. Make my work fruitful so I can celebrate in Your harvest. . . .

PRAYER REQUESTS

PRAISES

ANSWERS TO PRAYER

FRIDAY, DECEMBER 13

*We are to be looking for the great hope and the coming
of our great God and the One Who saves, Christ Jesus.*
TITUS 2:13 NLV

I take great comfort in that fact that You are the only one who can save me, Jesus.
I don't have to wonder if I've made the right choice. I am confident. I am sure. I
stand on the hope You have placed in my heart, and I know You are preparing a
place for me to live with You forever. . . .

PRAYER REQUESTS

ANSWERS
TO PRAYER

PRAISES

SATURDAY, DECEMBER 14

Be happy in your hope. Do not give up when trouble comes. Do not let anything stop you from praying.
ROMANS 12:12 NLV

Hope is the thing that gets me through a time of waiting, God. Sometimes, it's what I desperately cling to and all I have when trouble comes. But I admit that prayer is often the thing that goes by the wayside when I am struggling. Today, I am committed to talking to You and sharing my concerns and frustrations. And then, I will listen. . . .

PRAYER REQUESTS

PRAISES

ANSWERS TO PRAYER

SUNDAY, DECEMBER 15

"Be dressed ready for service and keep your lamps burning, like servants waiting for their master to return from a wedding banquet, so that when he comes and knocks they can immediately open the door for him."

LUKE 12:35–36 NIV

I am ready and waiting for You to act, Lord. I will not forget Your promise to show up at just the right time. Keep me vigilant, always looking for You so I can see You in even the smallest details. . . .

PRAYER REQUESTS

ANSWERS TO PRAYER

PRAISES

MONDAY, DECEMBER 16

If we look forward to something we don't yet have,
we must wait patiently and confidently.

ROMANS 8:25 NLT

Father, I love looking forward to good things. That's the hope I have in You. Help me to dream big dreams that are in line with Your plan for my life. And I am sure You will make those dreams become reality. Help me to be patient and to understand that You will make them happen in the time and way that is best for me. . . .

PRAYER REQUESTS

PRAISES

ANSWERS TO PRAYER

TUESDAY, DECEMBER 17

"Therefore do not worry about tomorrow, for tomorrow will worry about itself. Each day has enough trouble of its own."
MATTHEW 6:34 NIV

You have given me today, Lord, and I will live in the now. I will not borrow anxiety from tomorrow by worrying today, but I will instead trust You with both. I will not let my fear of the unknown overtake my faith in Your goodness. You are my strength and the melody in my heart. . . .

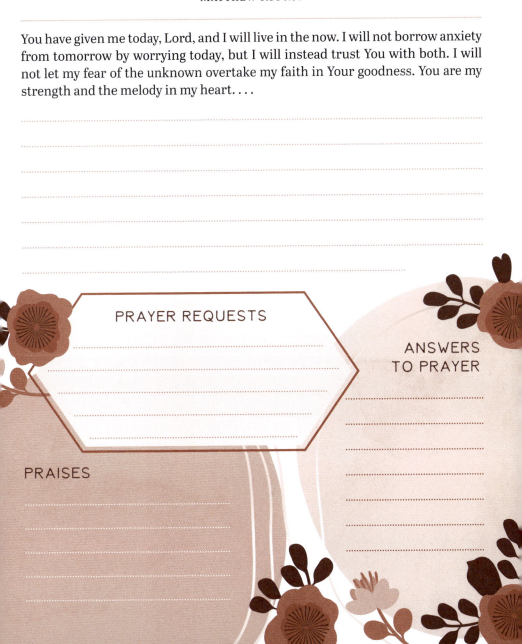

PRAYER REQUESTS

ANSWERS TO PRAYER

PRAISES

WEDNESDAY, DECEMBER 18

The Lord is not slow in keeping his promise, as some understand slowness. Instead he is patient with you.
2 Peter 3:9 NIV

Father God, thank You for being so patient with me. You encourage me to grow in my faith, but often I am slow to learn. In Your kindness, You show me how to become more like You, but still I sin and fall short of Your perfection. Yet, You shower me with Your grace and invite me to rise. . . .

PRAYER REQUESTS

PRAISES

ANSWERS TO PRAYER

THURSDAY, DECEMBER 19

So humble yourselves under the mighty power of God,
and at the right time he will lift you up in honor.

1 PETER 5:6 NLT

God, I cannot understand Your greatness fully. And when I think about how mighty and powerful You are, I realize how small I am. Thank You for being a gigantic God who takes care of all Your creation. Show me my role in Your plan, and let me be an integral part of all of creation glorifying You. . . .

PRAYER REQUESTS

ANSWERS TO PRAYER

PRAISES

FRIDAY, DECEMBER 20

*We give great honor to those who endure under suffering.
For instance, you know about Job, a man of great
endurance. You can see how the Lord was kind to him at
the end, for the Lord is full of tenderness and mercy.*

JAMES 5:11 NLT

Almighty Lord, please show me Your kindness when I go through a difficult season of waiting. Refine me and strengthen me to better understand Your ways and plan for me, and give me patience to endure. . . .

PRAYER REQUESTS

PRAISES

ANSWERS TO PRAYER

SATURDAY, DECEMBER 21

First Day of Winter

"Therefore the Lord Himself shall give you a sign. Behold, a virgin shall conceive and bear a son and shall call His name Immanuel."
ISAIAH 7:14 SKJV

Lord, evidence of Your work is all around me, but while I am waiting for answers, I am sometimes blind to see Your work now. Open my eyes to see the wonderful things You are doing, and give me confidence in the steps You will lead me through in the future. . . .

PRAYER REQUESTS

ANSWERS TO PRAYER

PRAISES

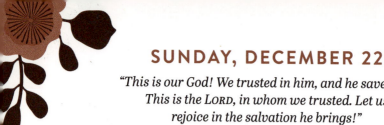

SUNDAY, DECEMBER 22

*"This is our God! We trusted in him, and he saved us!
This is the LORD, in whom we trusted. Let us
rejoice in the salvation he brings!"*

ISAIAH 25:9 NLT

I trust You, Father. At just the right time, You sent Your Son to earth. At just the right time, You performed a miracle where a virgin girl gave birth to Him. At just the right time, You started His journey to the cross. At just the right time, You raised Him from the dead. . . .

PRAYER REQUESTS

PRAISES

ANSWERS TO PRAYER

MONDAY, DECEMBER 23

Mary responded, "I am the Lord's servant.
May everything you have said about me come true."
LUKE 1:38 NLT

Lord, thank You for the example Mary set. I am listening intently to hear what You say about my future. Like Mary, I am praying that everything You say about me comes true. I am Your servant, Father. Your ways are perfect, including Your ways for me. I trust Your timing in all things. I am a willing vessel for You. . . .

PRAYER REQUESTS

ANSWERS
TO PRAYER

PRAISES

TUESDAY, DECEMBER 24

Christmas Eve

While they were there, the time came for the baby to be born.

LUKE 2:6 NIV

What was it like for You to see Your Son be born, Father? You live outside time, yet You are in charge of all time. You knew exactly when Jesus would come to earth as a baby. You wove together the strands of history to that precise manger scene in Bethlehem; and through Jesus' life, death, and resurrection, You ushered in salvation. Glory to God in the highest! . . .

PRAYER REQUESTS

PRAISES

ANSWERS TO PRAYER

Mary treasured up all these things and pondered them in her heart.
LUKE 2:19 NIV

Jesus, Your presence is all around me—especially at Christmas. Thank You for willingly stepping down from heaven to come to earth as a baby to live life both fully God and fully human. Open my eyes to see You and praise You for all You are: Master, Savior, and Friend. I will treasure these truths in my heart and honor the meaning of Christmas throughout the year. . . .

PRAYER REQUESTS

ANSWERS TO PRAYER

PRAISES

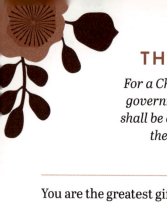

THURSDAY, DECEMBER 26

For a Child is born to us, a Son is given to us, and the government shall be on His shoulder. And His name shall be called Wonderful, Counselor, the Mighty God, the Everlasting Father, the Prince of Peace.

ISAIAH 9:6 SKJV

You are the greatest gift I have ever received, Jesus, and I want to shine Your light of hope into the dark world. You are wonderful. You are mighty. You and the Father are one. I welcome Your presence in my life, today and always. . . .

PRAYER REQUESTS

PRAISES

ANSWERS TO PRAYER

FRIDAY, DECEMBER 27

*"Glory to God in the highest, and on
earth peace, goodwill toward men."*
LUKE 2:14 SKJV

After waiting for so long for the Savior to be born, it's no wonder the angels
sang such a loud, joyful chorus to the shepherds! Let my praise of You, God, be
as heartfelt. All glory belongs to You because Your timing is perfect. Your ways
are good. Your love is all-encompassing. And Your grace covers every one of my
sins! . . .

PRAYER REQUESTS

ANSWERS
TO PRAYER

PRAISES

SATURDAY, DECEMBER 28

May the God of hope fill you with all joy and peace as you trust in him,
so that you may overflow with hope by the power of the Holy Spirit.
ROMANS 15:13 NIV

You are the God of hope, Father. Your hope isn't a mystical wish that everything will be okay. The hope I have in You is steadfast—grounded in the promises You have fulfilled in the Bible and in my own life. Increase my faith so that my hope will grow as well. . . .

PRAYER REQUESTS

PRAISES

ANSWERS TO PRAYER

SUNDAY, DECEMBER 29

God blesses those who patiently endure testing and temptation. Afterward they will receive the crown of life that God has promised to those who love him.

JAMES 1:12 NLT

When I am tested and tempted, Lord, provide me with an extra dose of Your strength. Be by my side and help me to resist and endure, because I know I can't do it alone. I love You, Lord, and I want my life to be a living sacrifice to You. . . .

PRAYER REQUESTS

ANSWERS TO PRAYER

PRAISES

MONDAY, DECEMBER 30

You open Your hand and fill the desire of every living thing.
PSALM 145:16 NLV

Lord God, I am thankful for Your blessings in my life. You make sure that I have enough to eat, that I have clothes to wear, that I am warm, and that I am afe. But You fill so much more than physical needs. You've given me a purpose and a spiritual family and an identity in You. I am worthy because You make me so. . . .

PRAYER REQUESTS

PRAISES

ANSWERS TO PRAYER

TUESDAY, DECEMBER 31

New Year's Eve

O Lord, let Your loving-kindness be upon us as we put our hope in You.
PSALM 33:22 NLV

Father, as I enter a new year, I humbly ask You to go before me in all things. I have confident hope in the things You will accomplish in 2025. Use me as You see fit. I am Your willing servant, and I trust You to shower me with Your goodness every step of the way. . . .

PRAYER REQUESTS

ANSWERS TO PRAYER

PRAISES

CONTRIBUTORS

JoAnne Simmons is a writer and editor who is in awe of God's love and the ways He guides and provides. Her favorite things include coffee shops, libraries, the Bible, good grammar, being a wife and mom, dogs, music, Disney World, punctuation, church, the beach, and many dear family and friends—but not in that order. If her family weren't so loving and flexible, she'd be in big trouble; and if God's mercies weren't new every morning, she'd never get out of bed. JoAnne wrote entries for February, March, May, July, September, and November.

Annie Tipton made up her first story at the ripe old age of two when she asked her mom to write it down for her. Since then, she has read and written many words as a student, newspaper reporter, author, and editor. She has a passion for making God's Word come alive for readers through devotions and Bible study. Annie loves snow (which is a good thing because she lives in Ohio), wearing scarves, eating sushi, playing Scrabble, and spending time with friends and family. Annie wrote entries for January, April, June, August, October, and December.